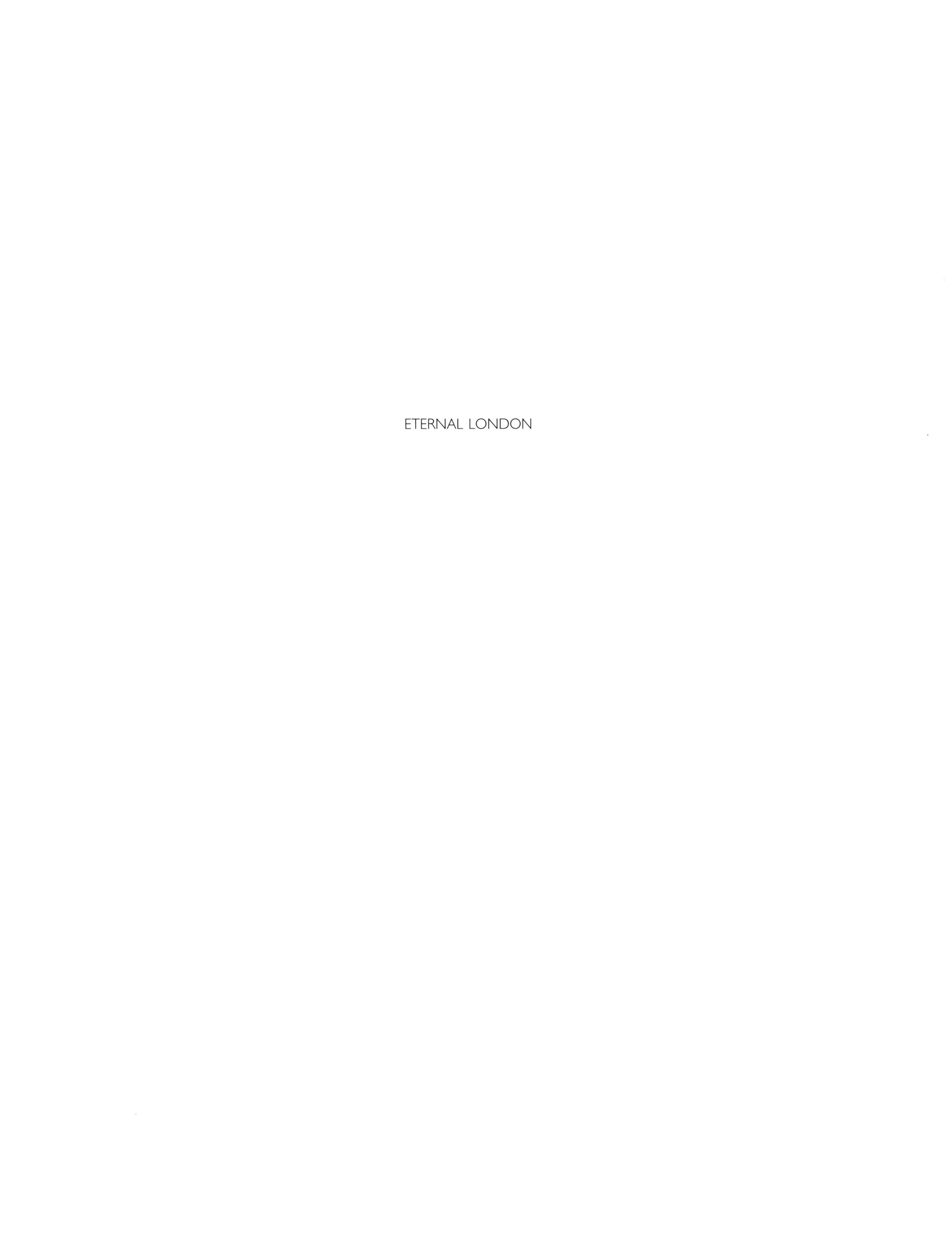

ETERNAL LONDON

GIACOMO BRUNELLI
ETERNAL LONDON

dewi lewis publishing

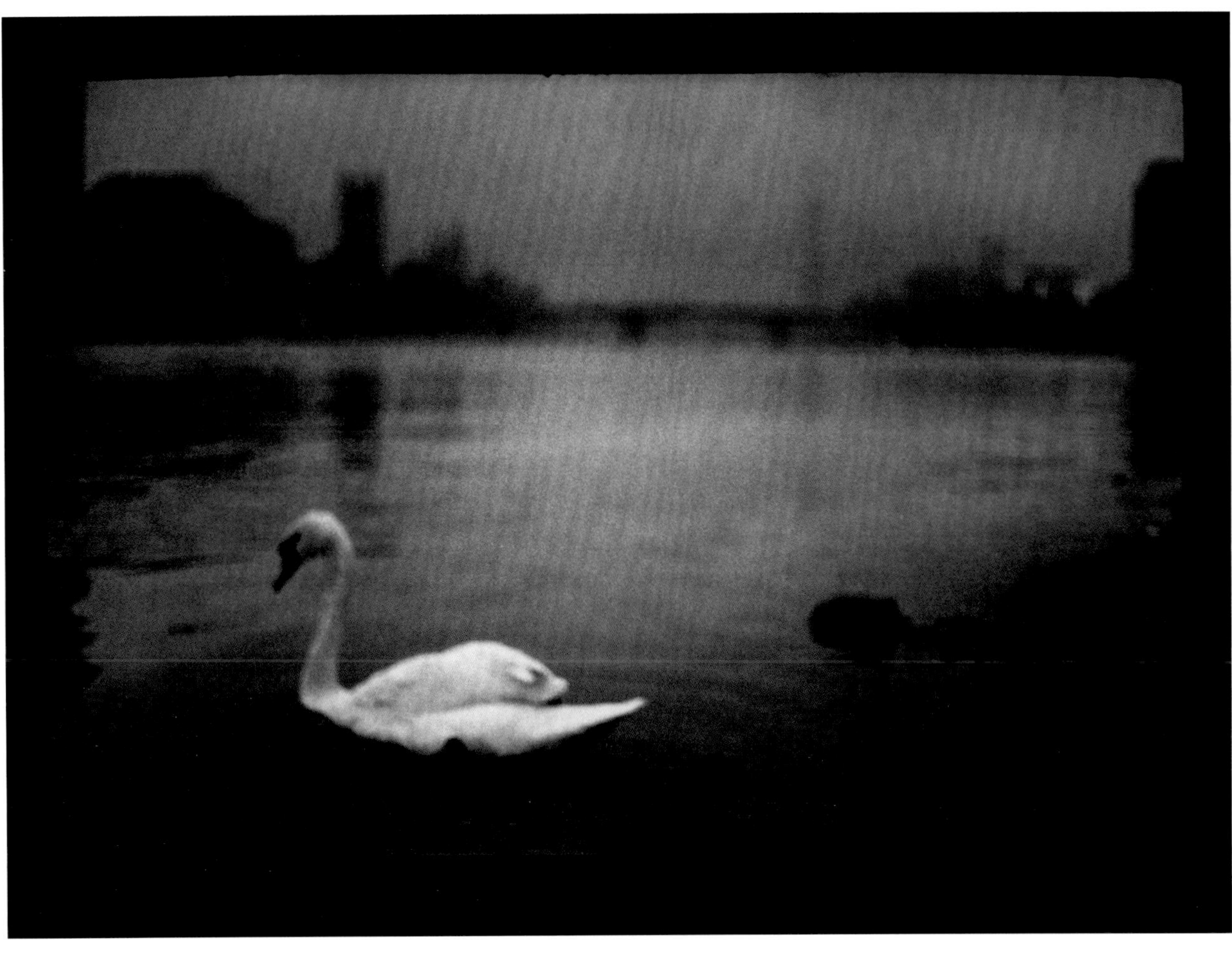

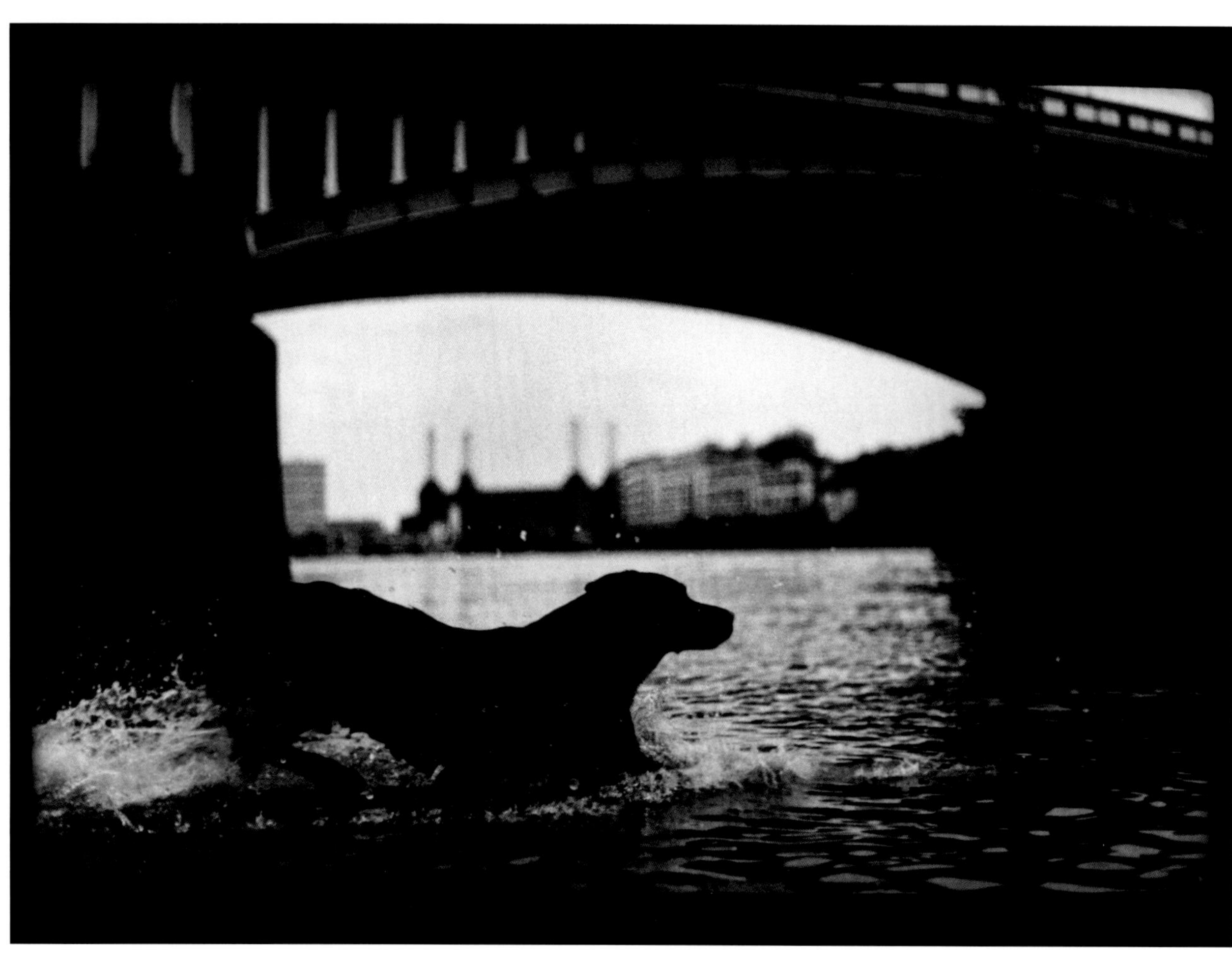

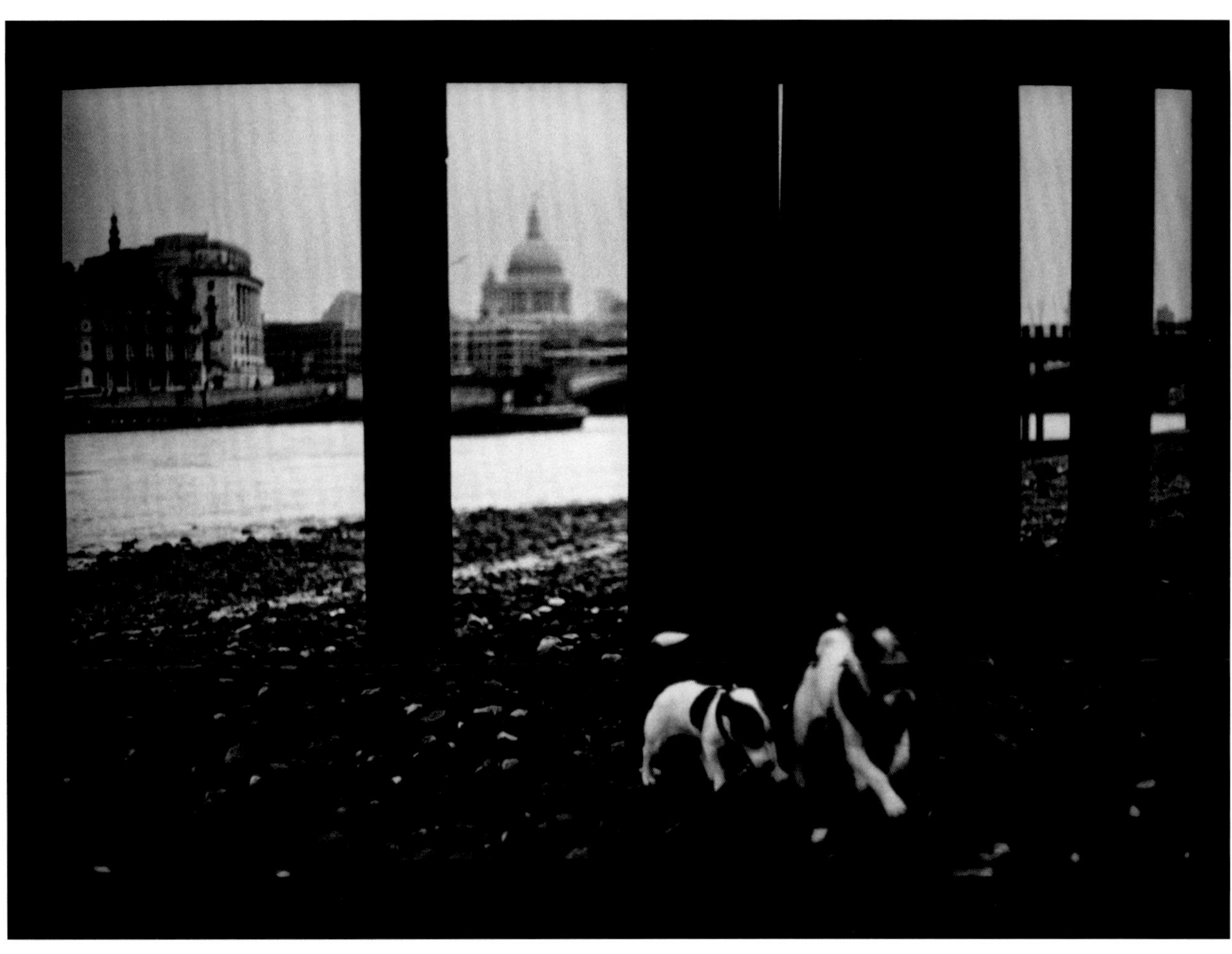

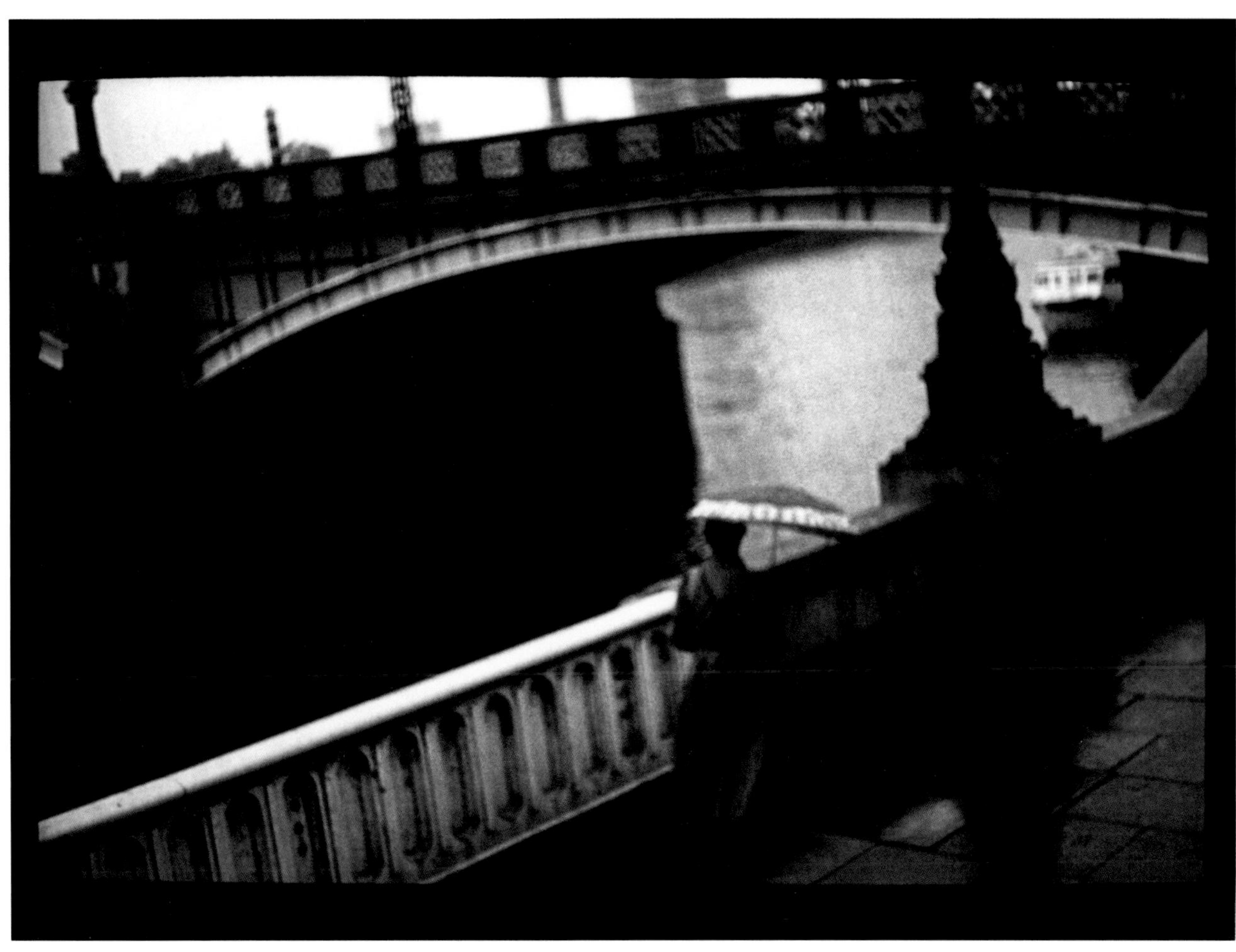

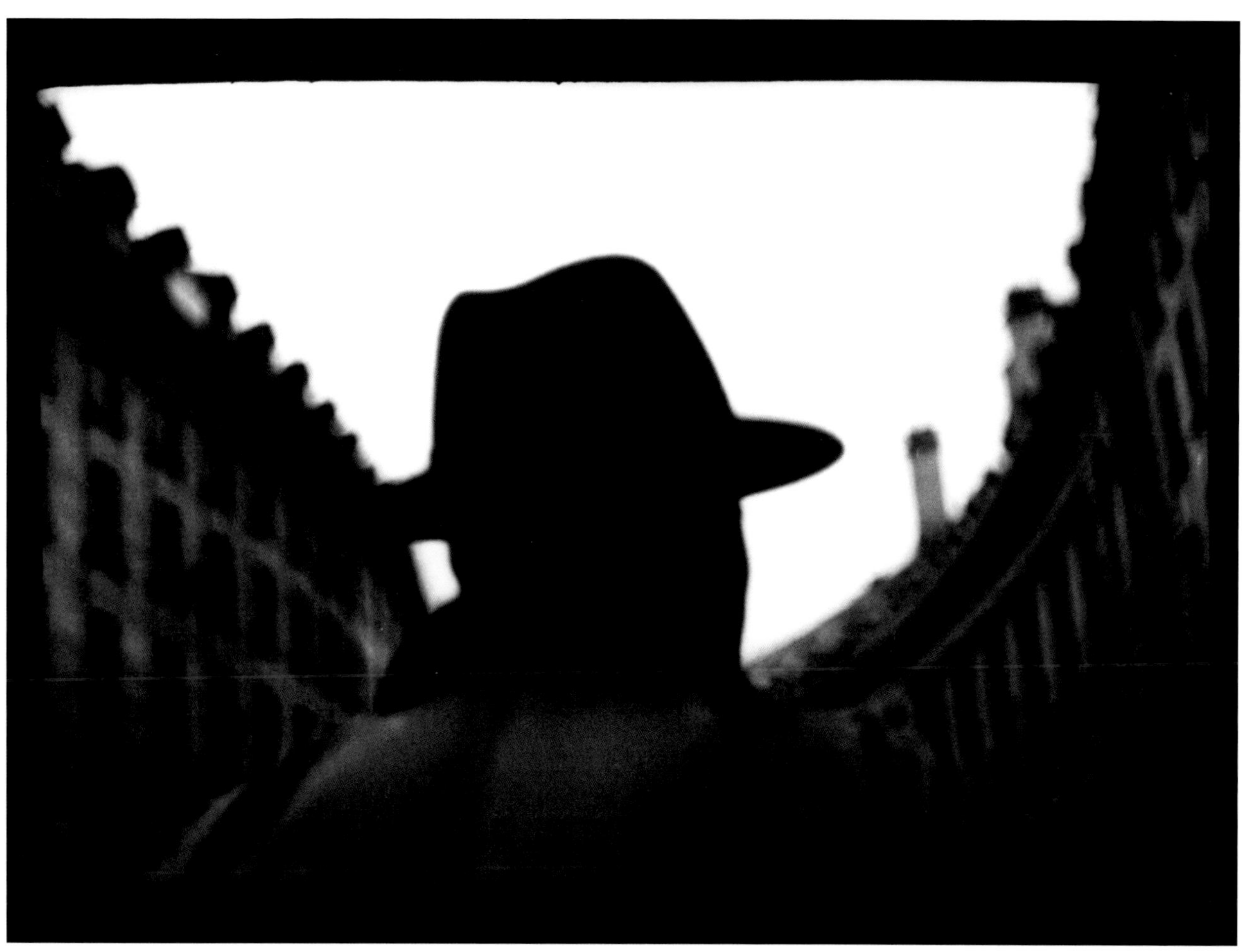

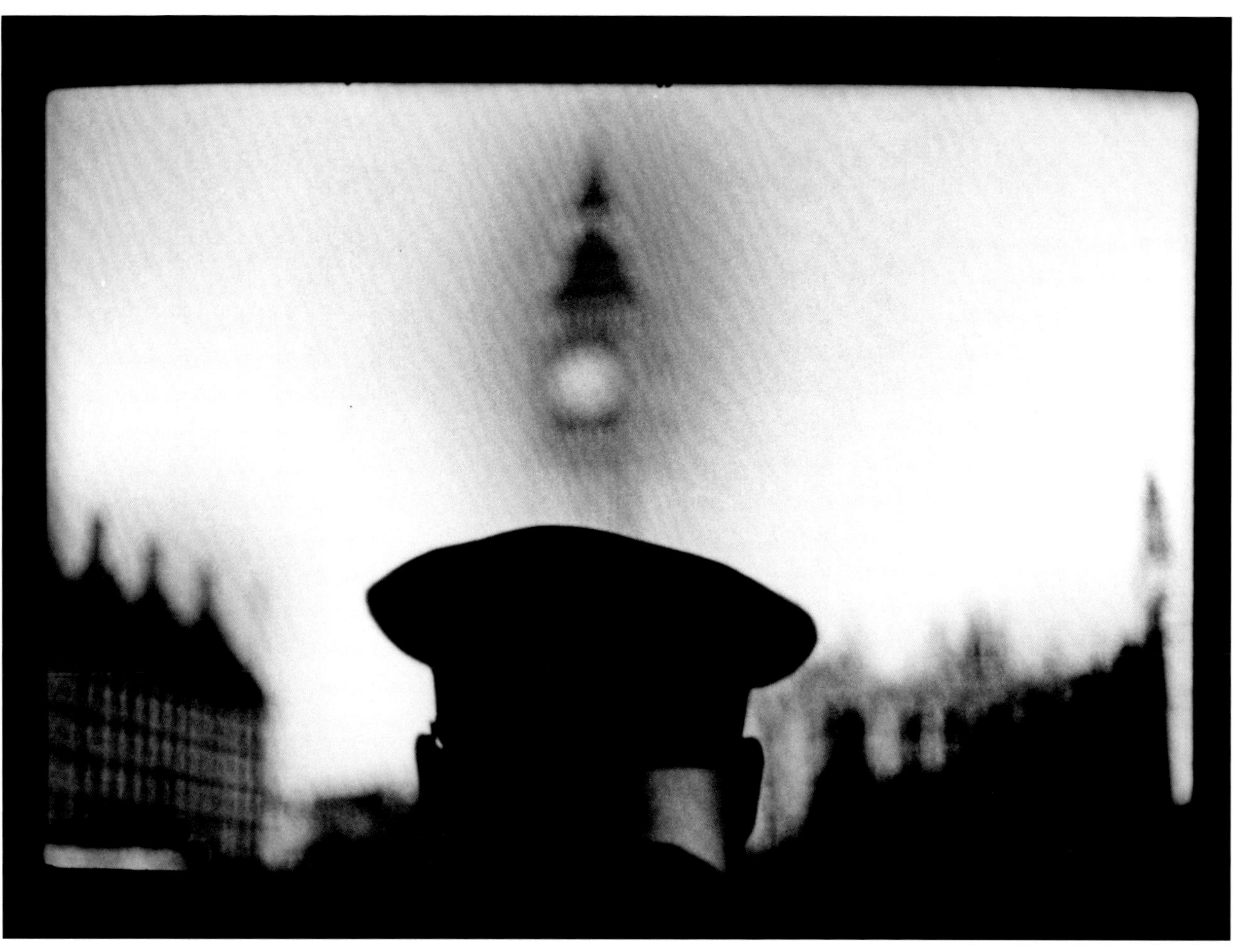

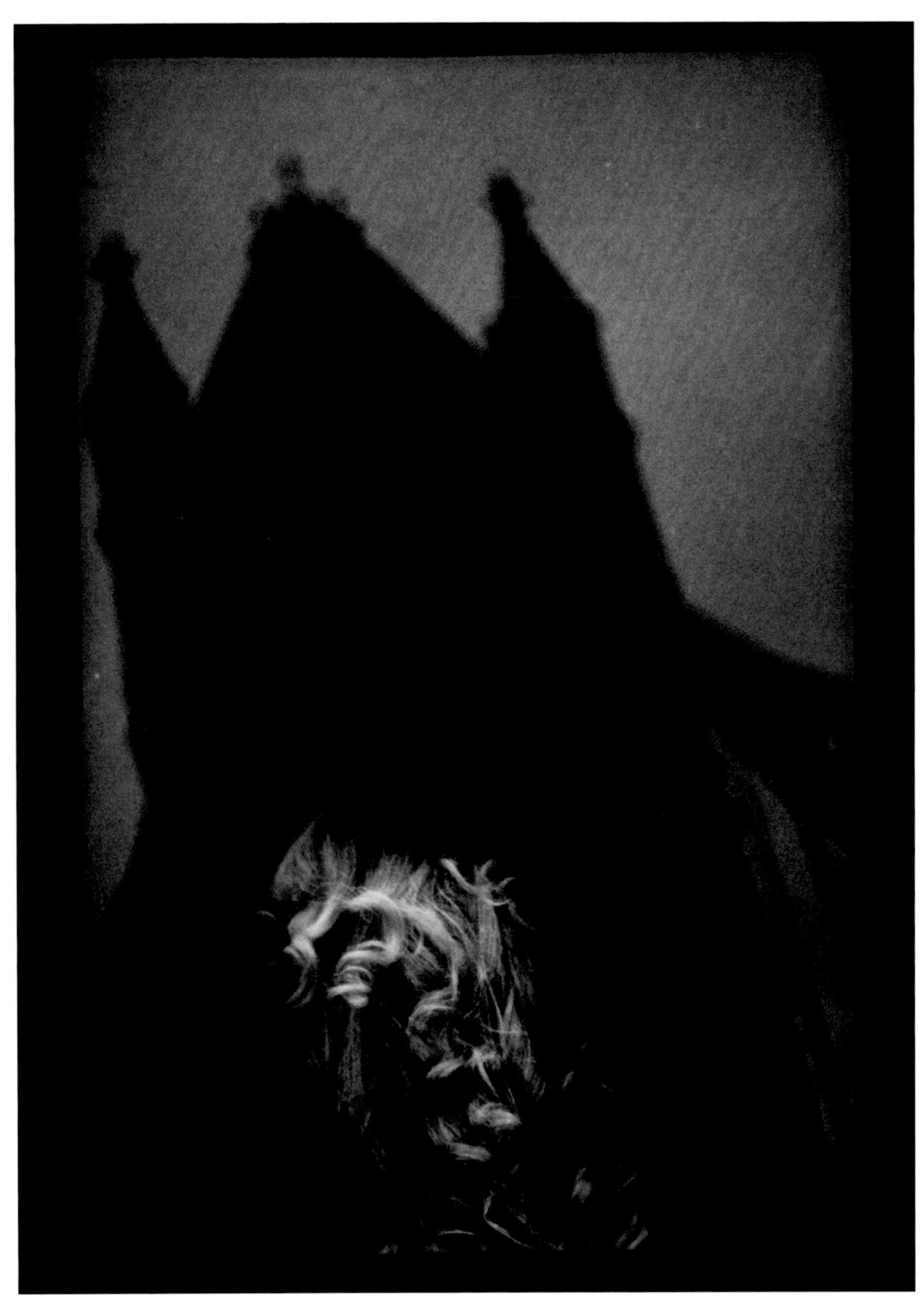

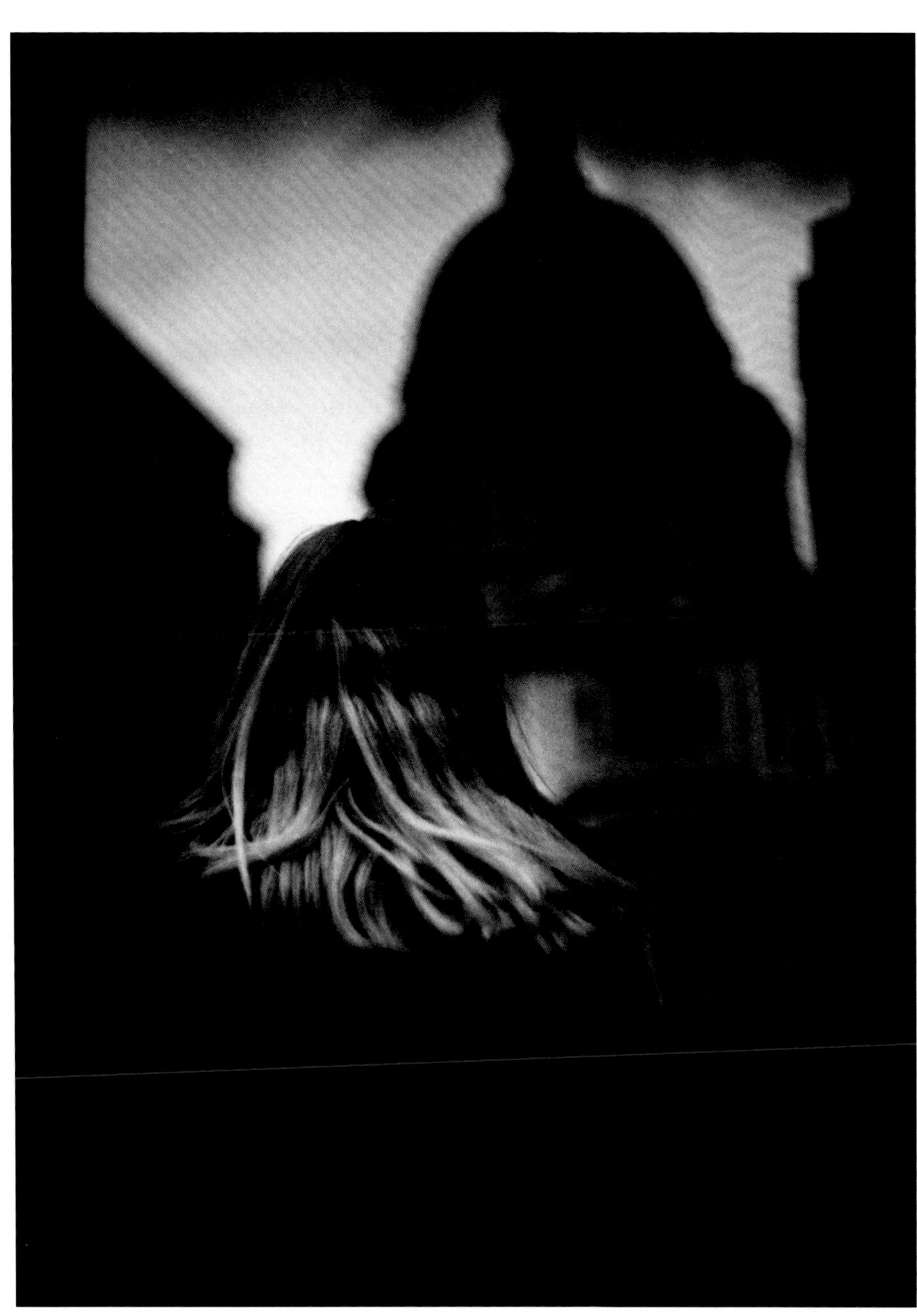

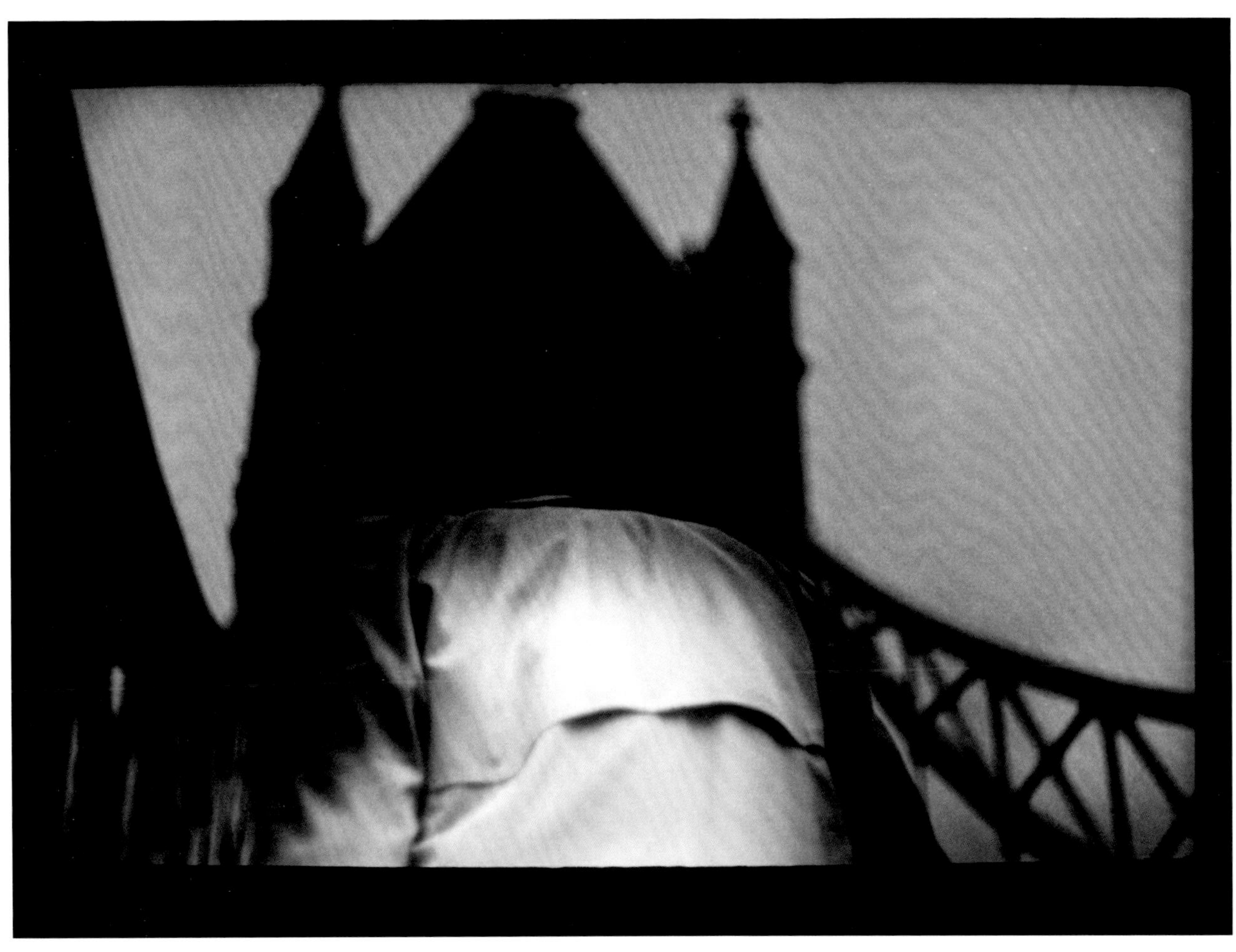

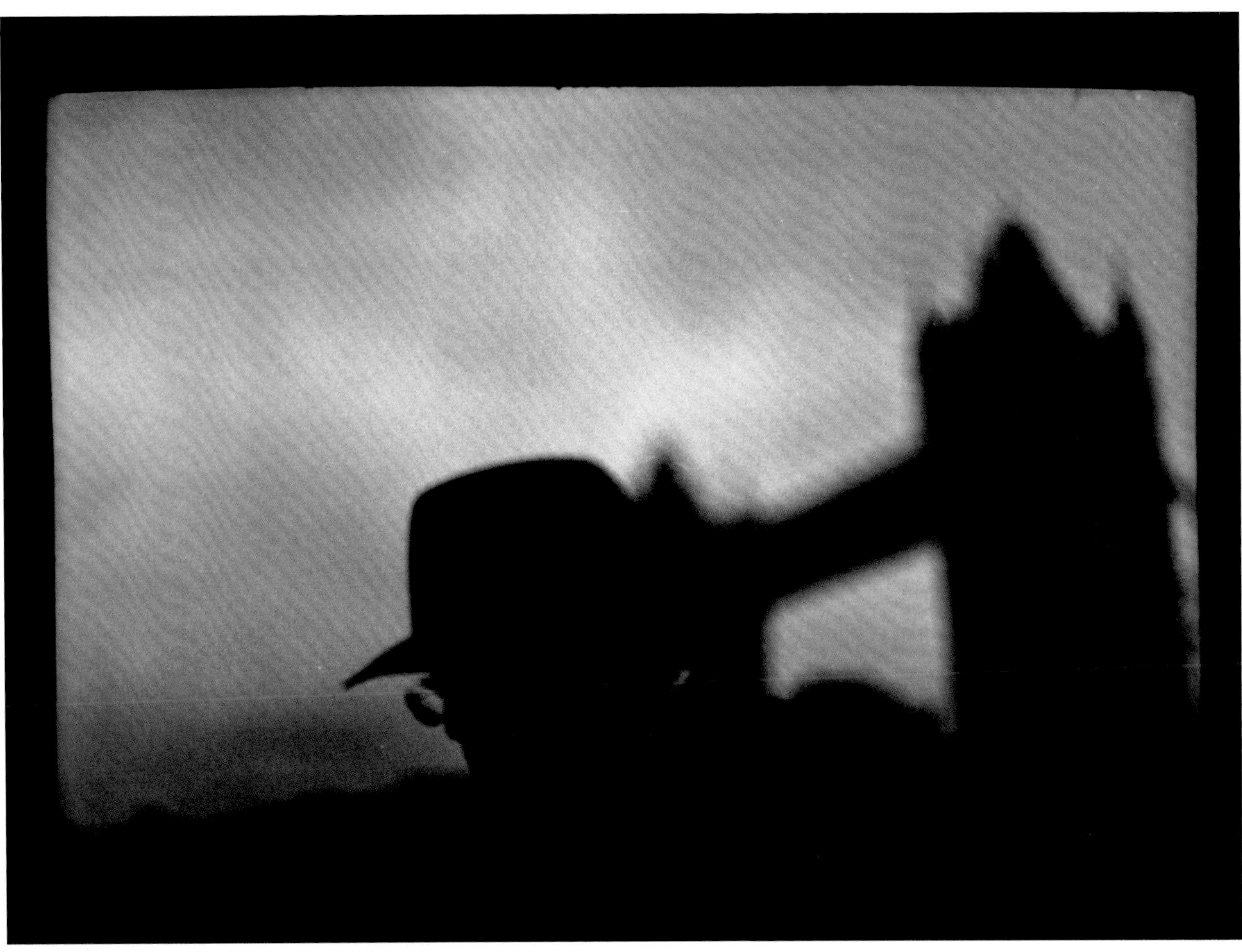

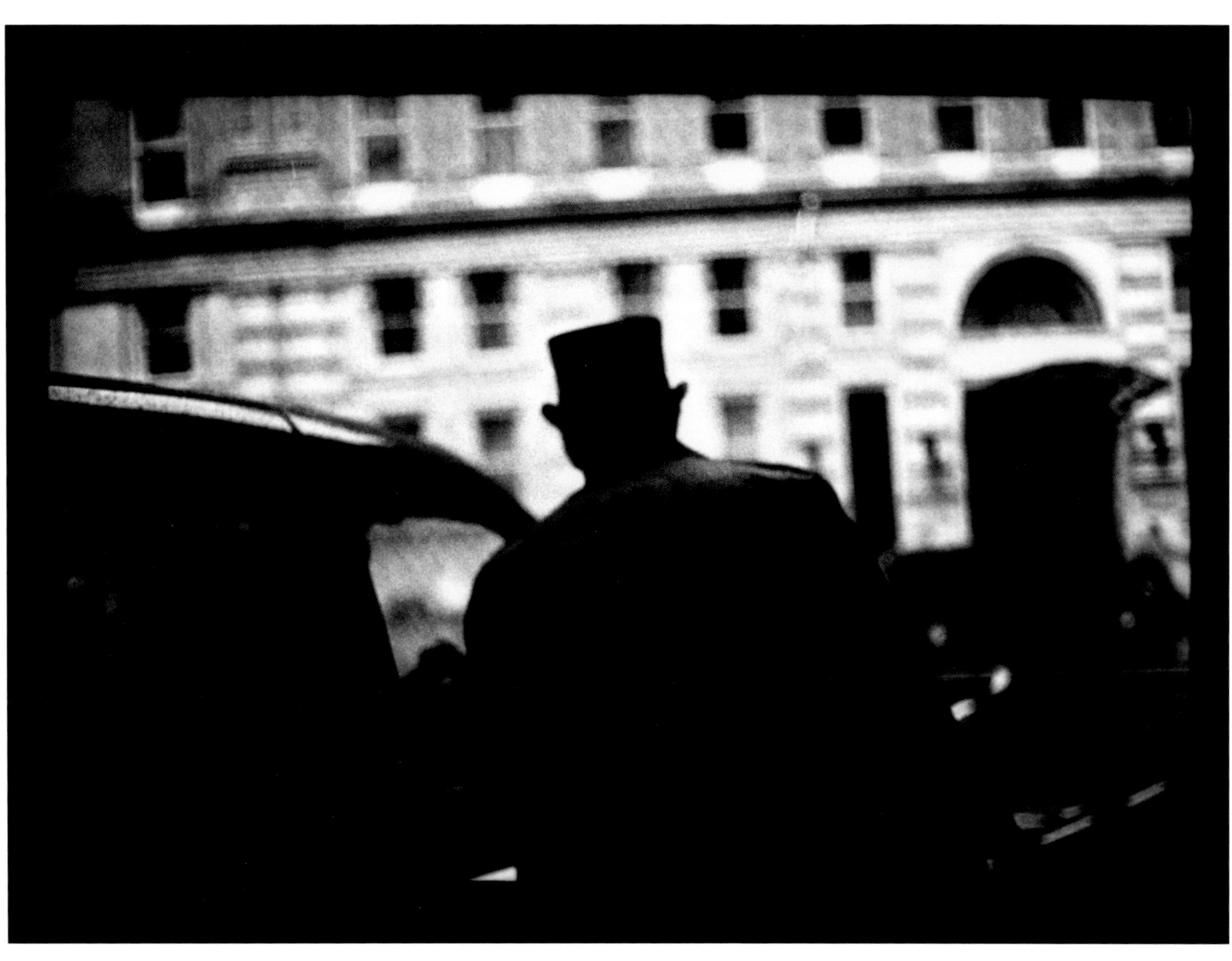

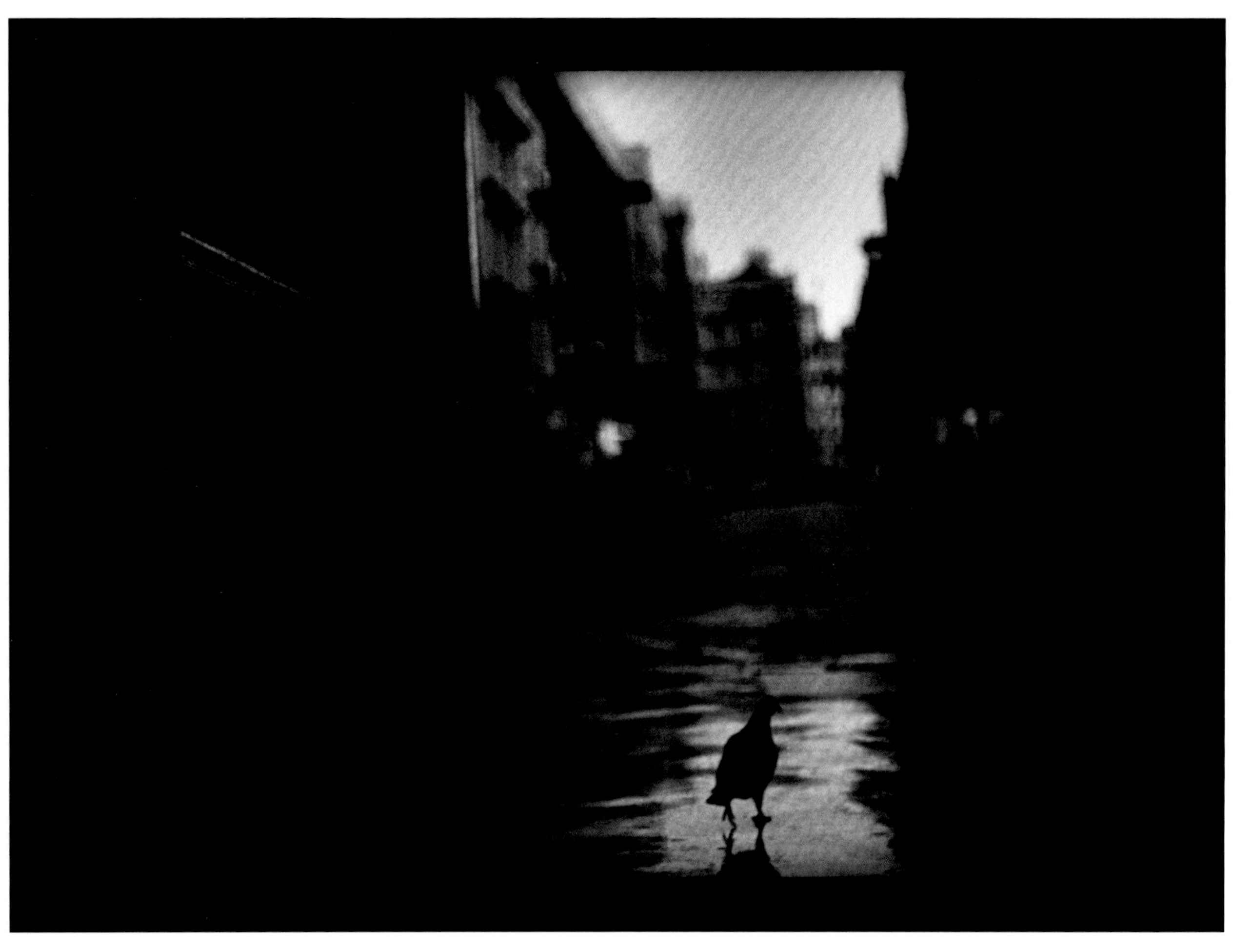

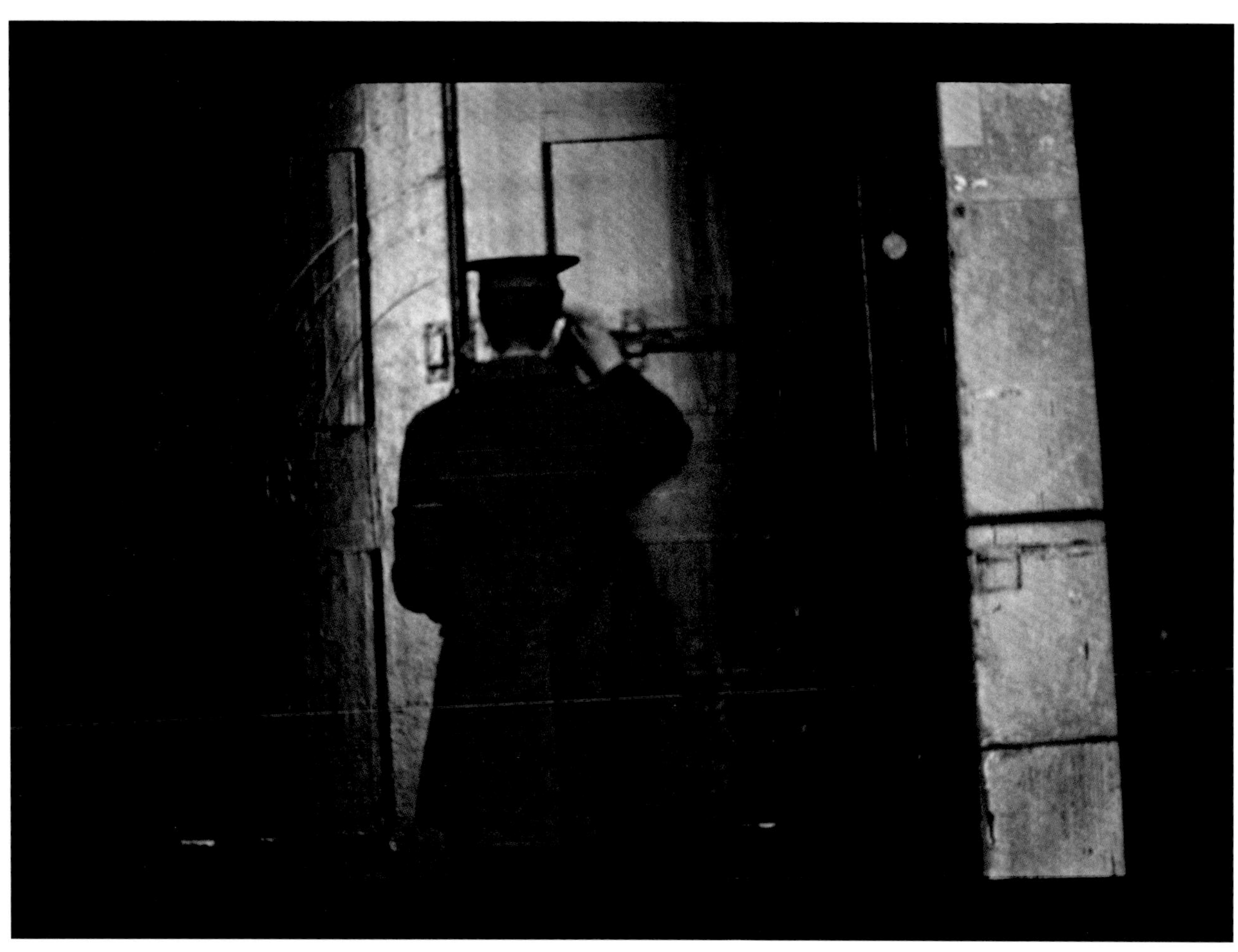

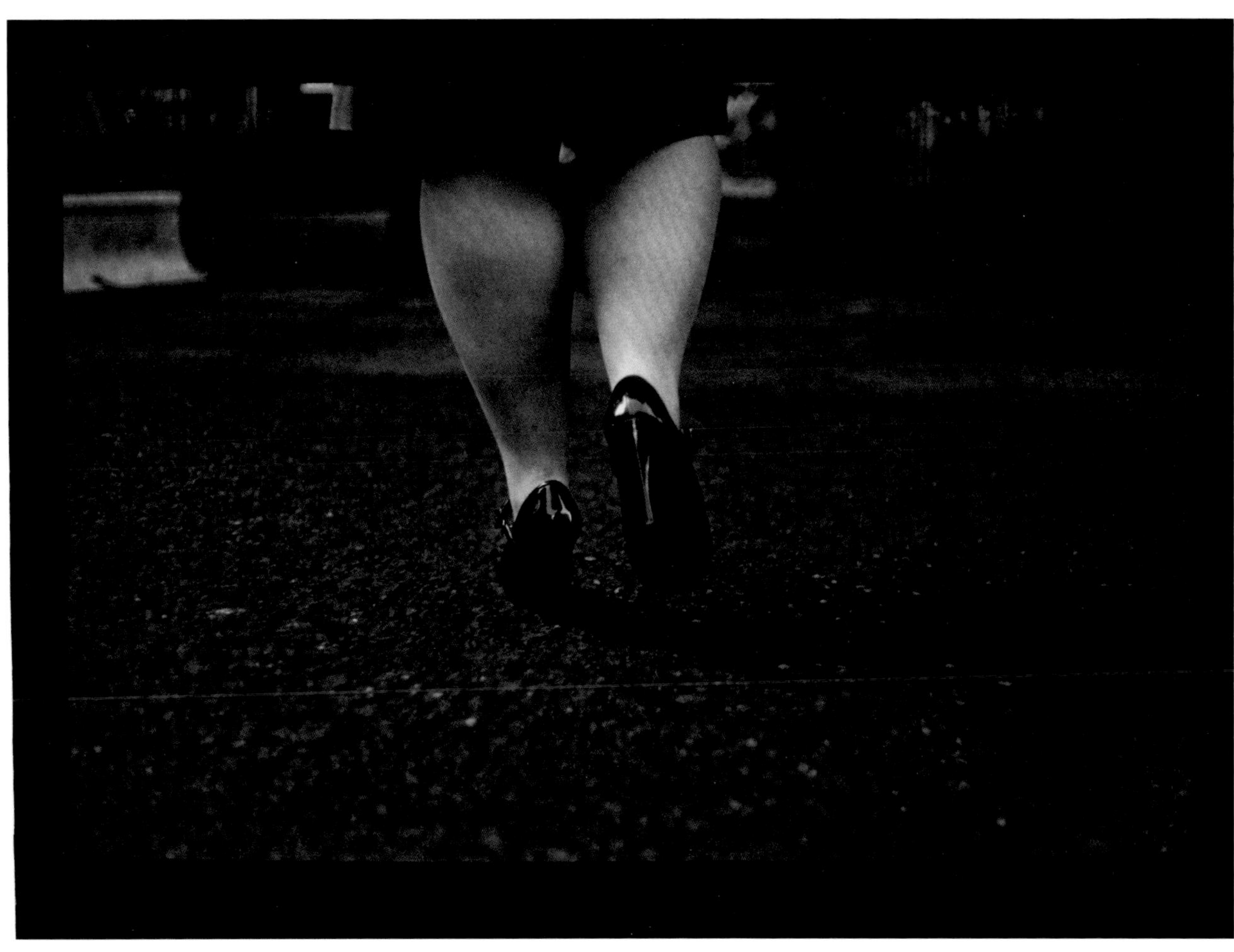

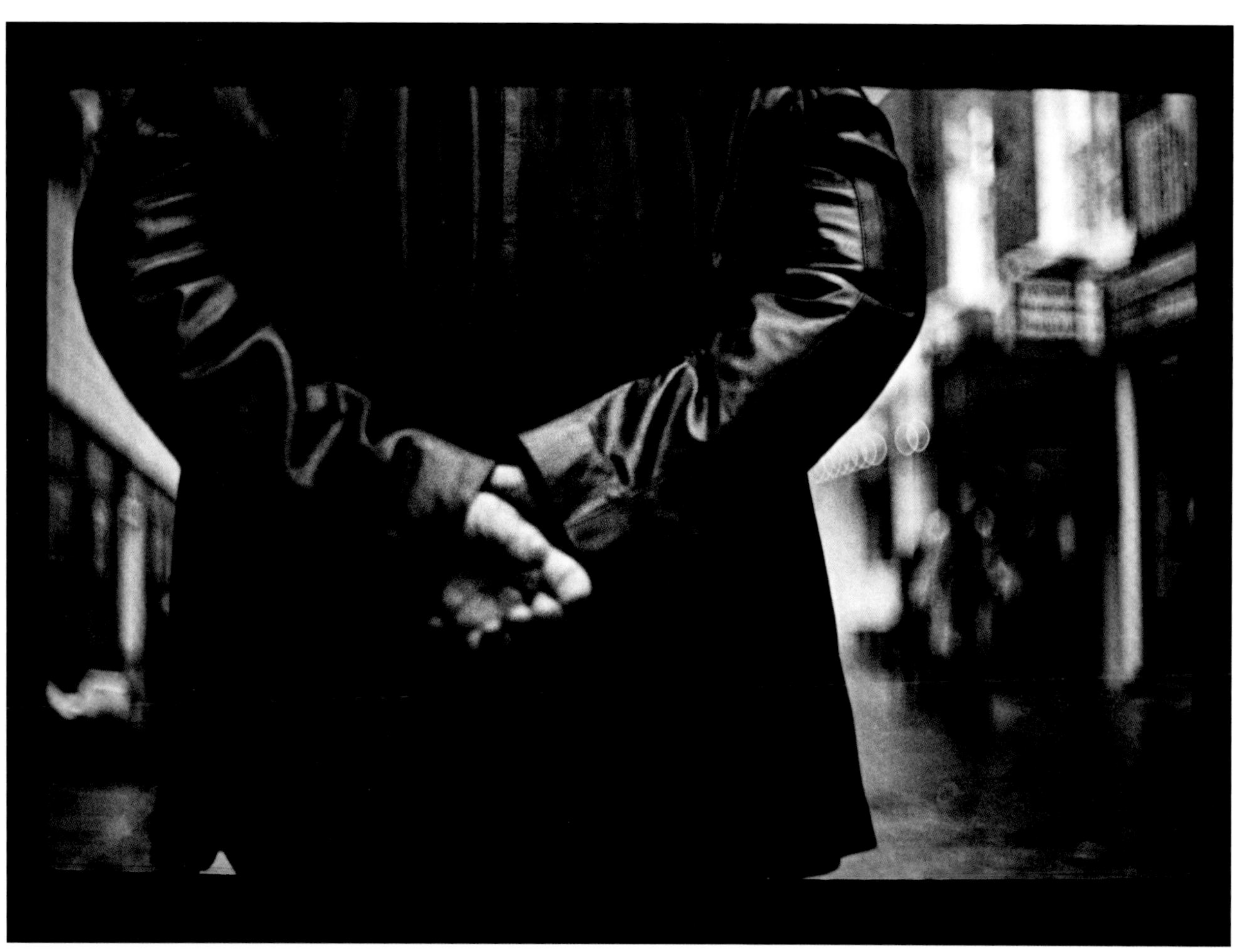

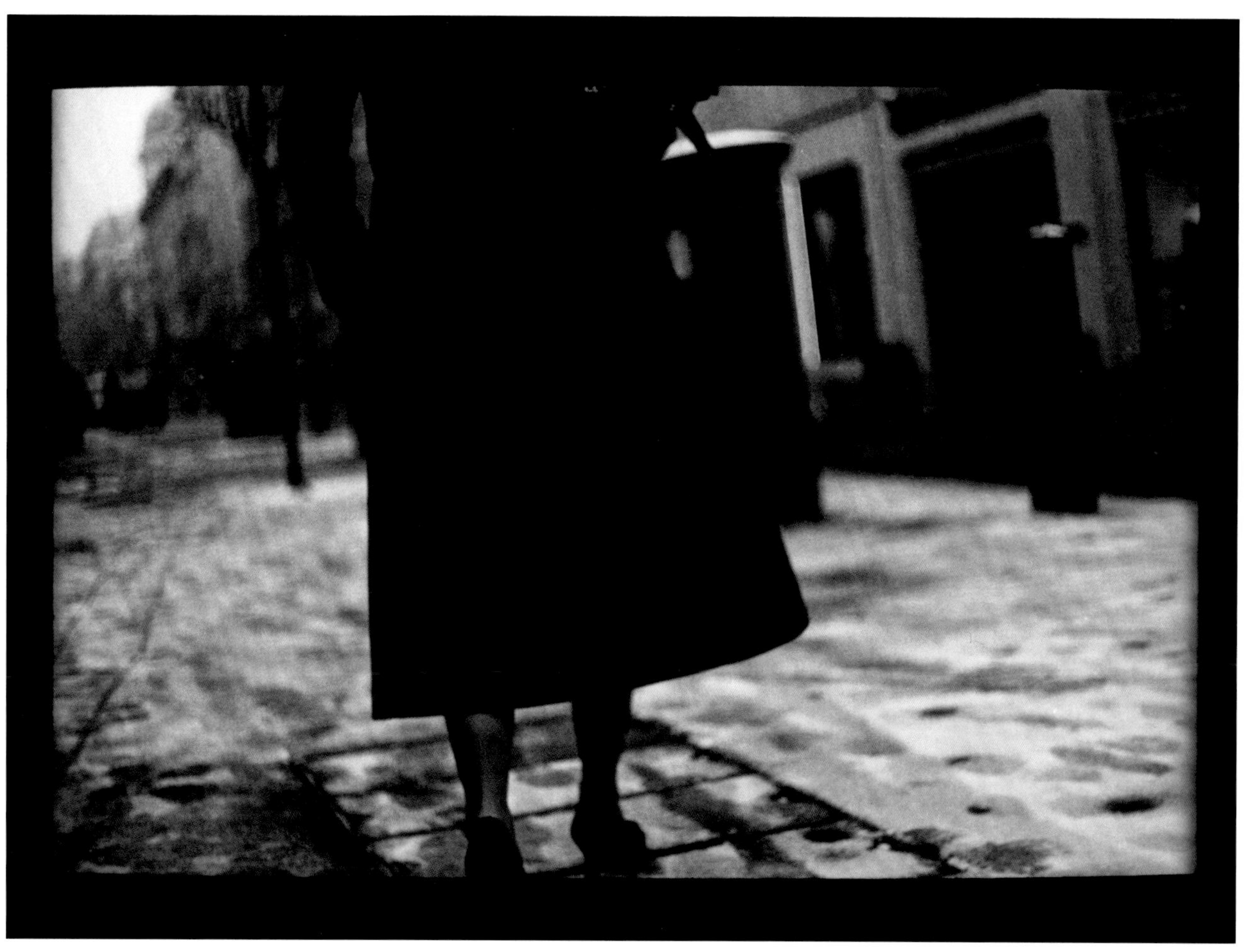

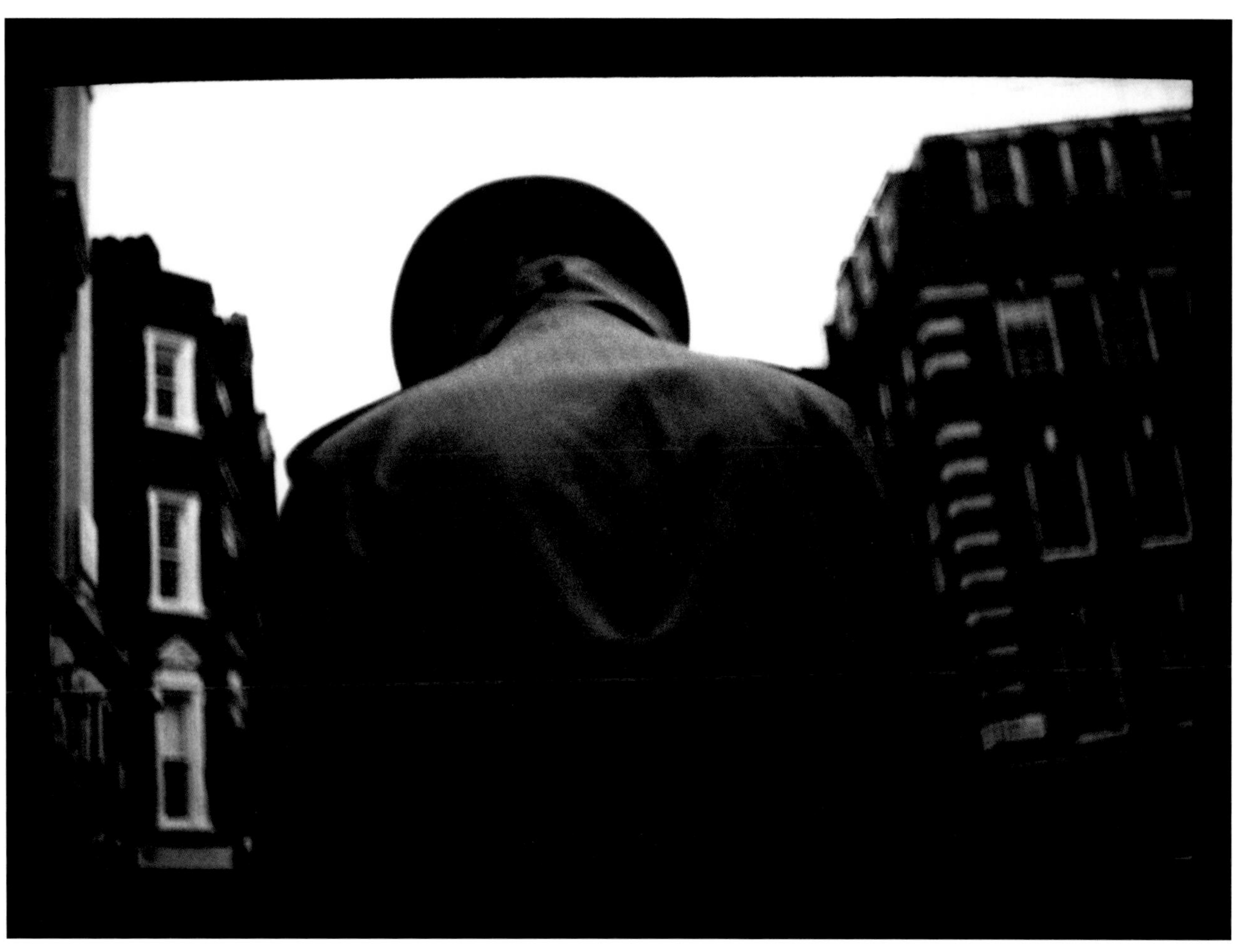

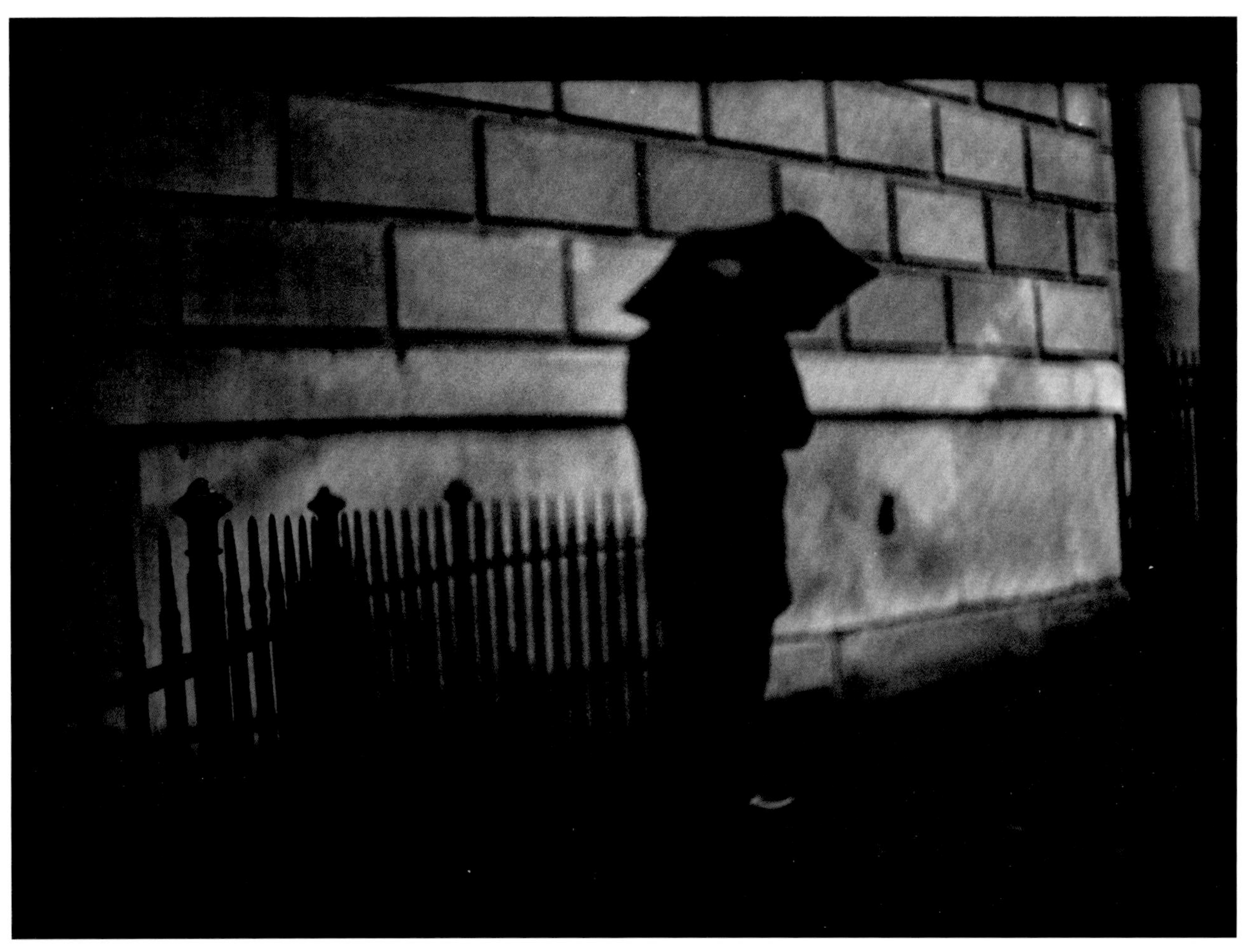

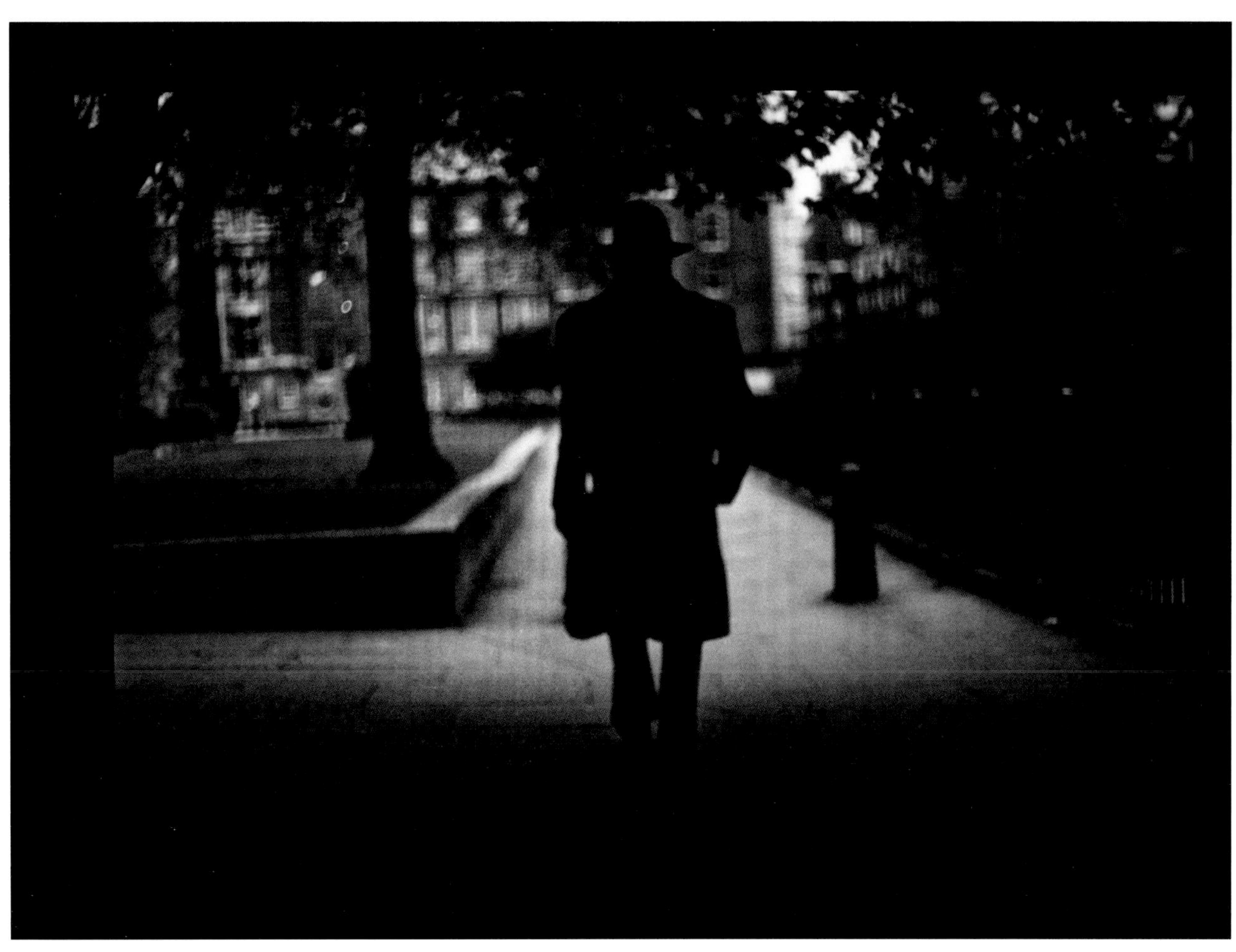

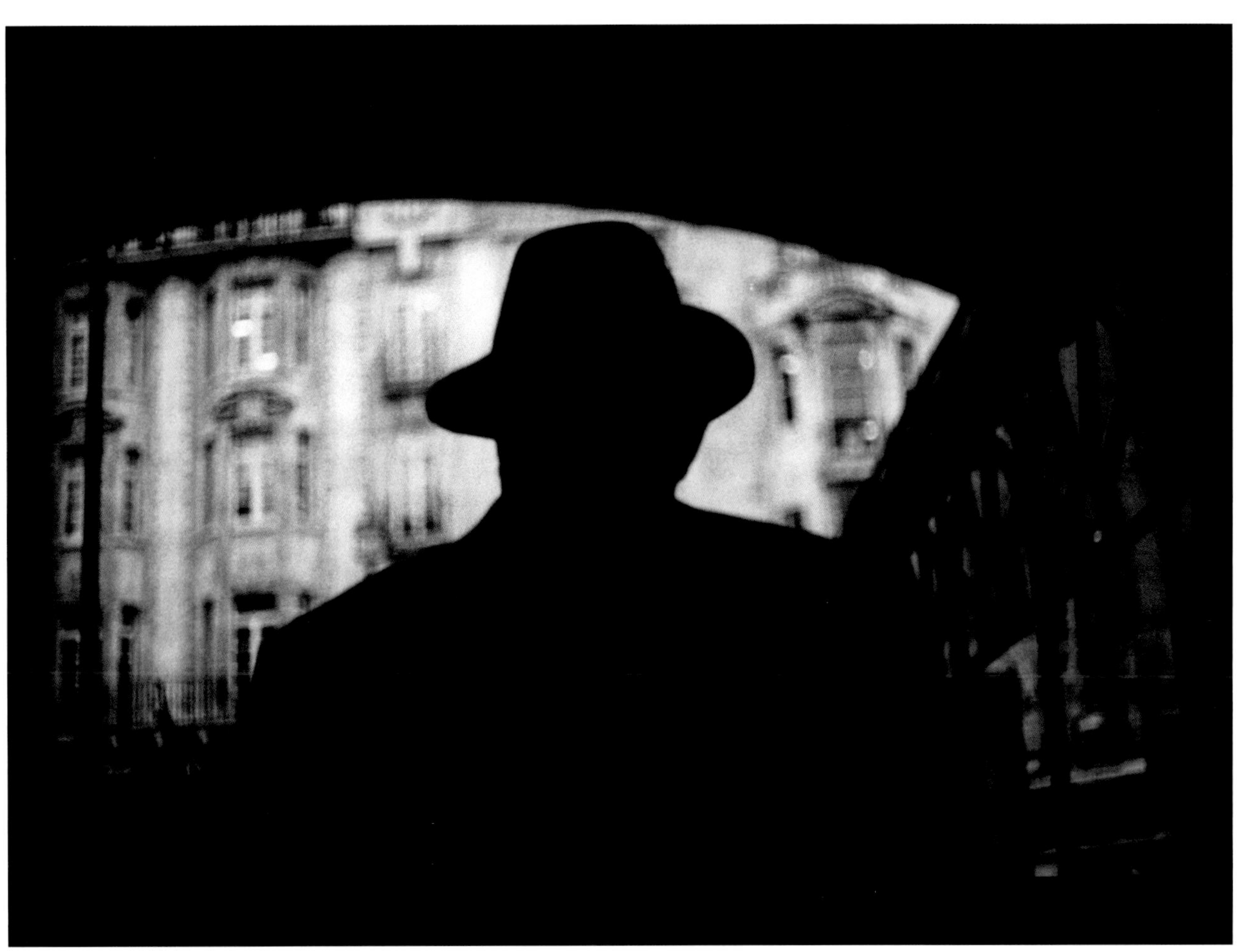

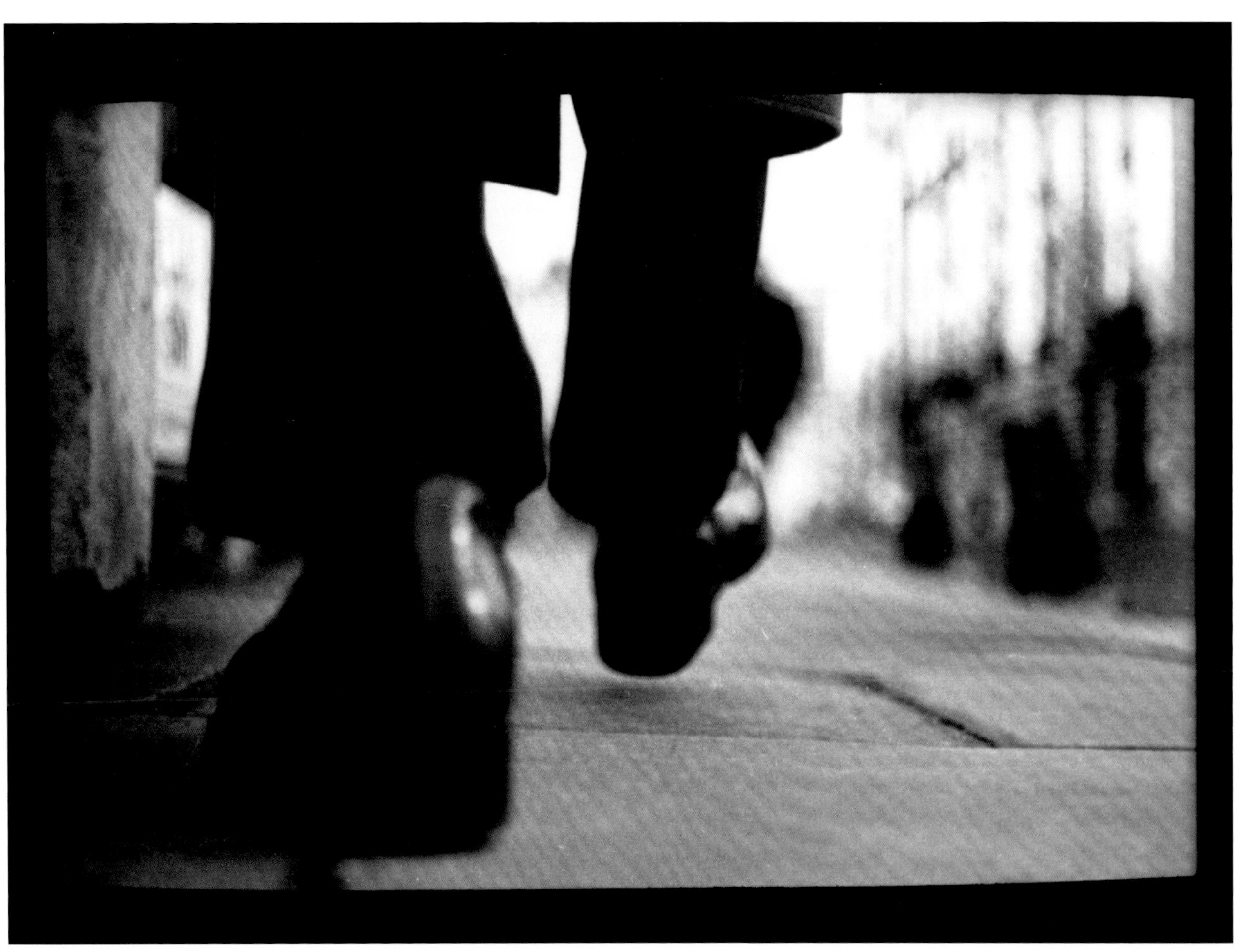

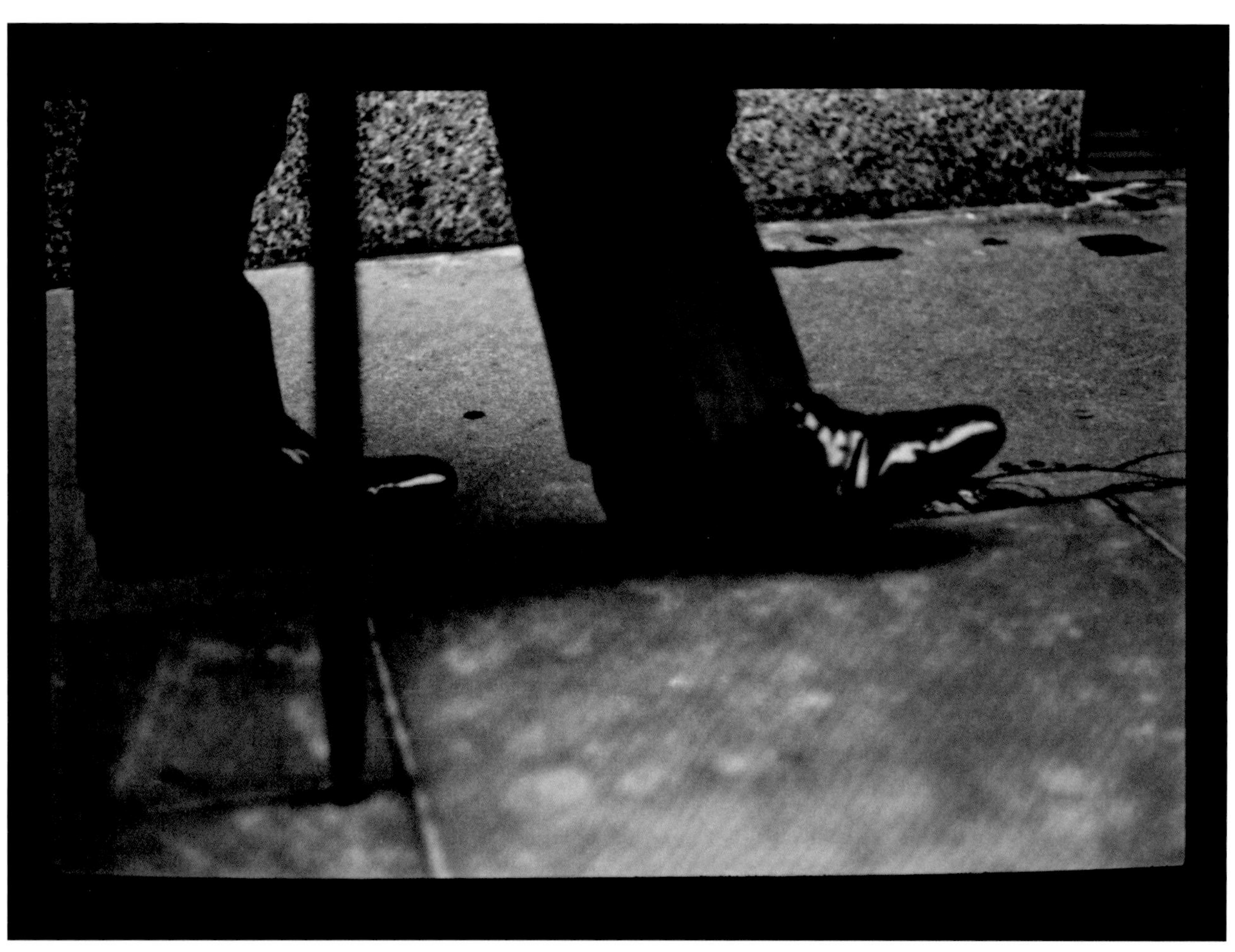

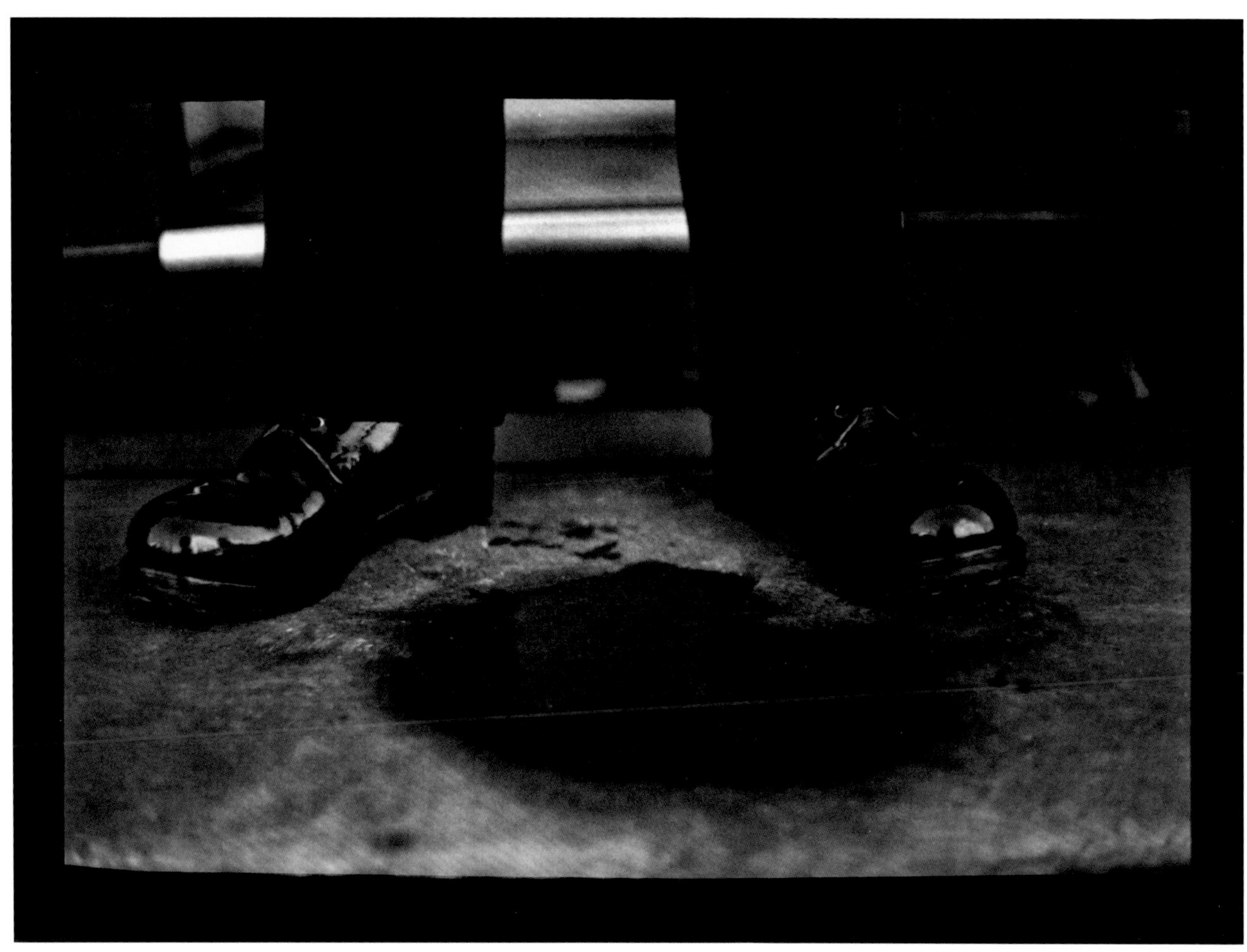

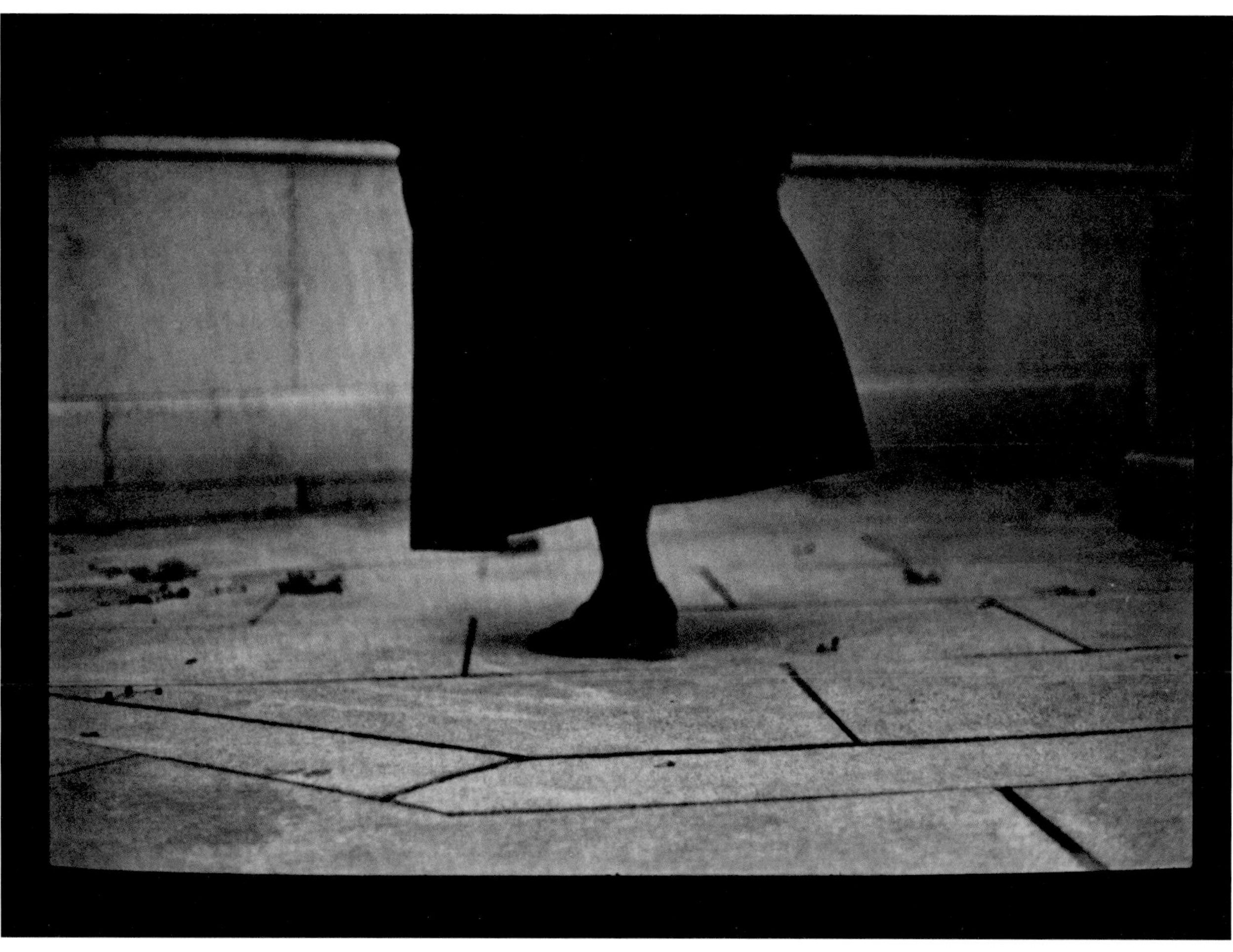

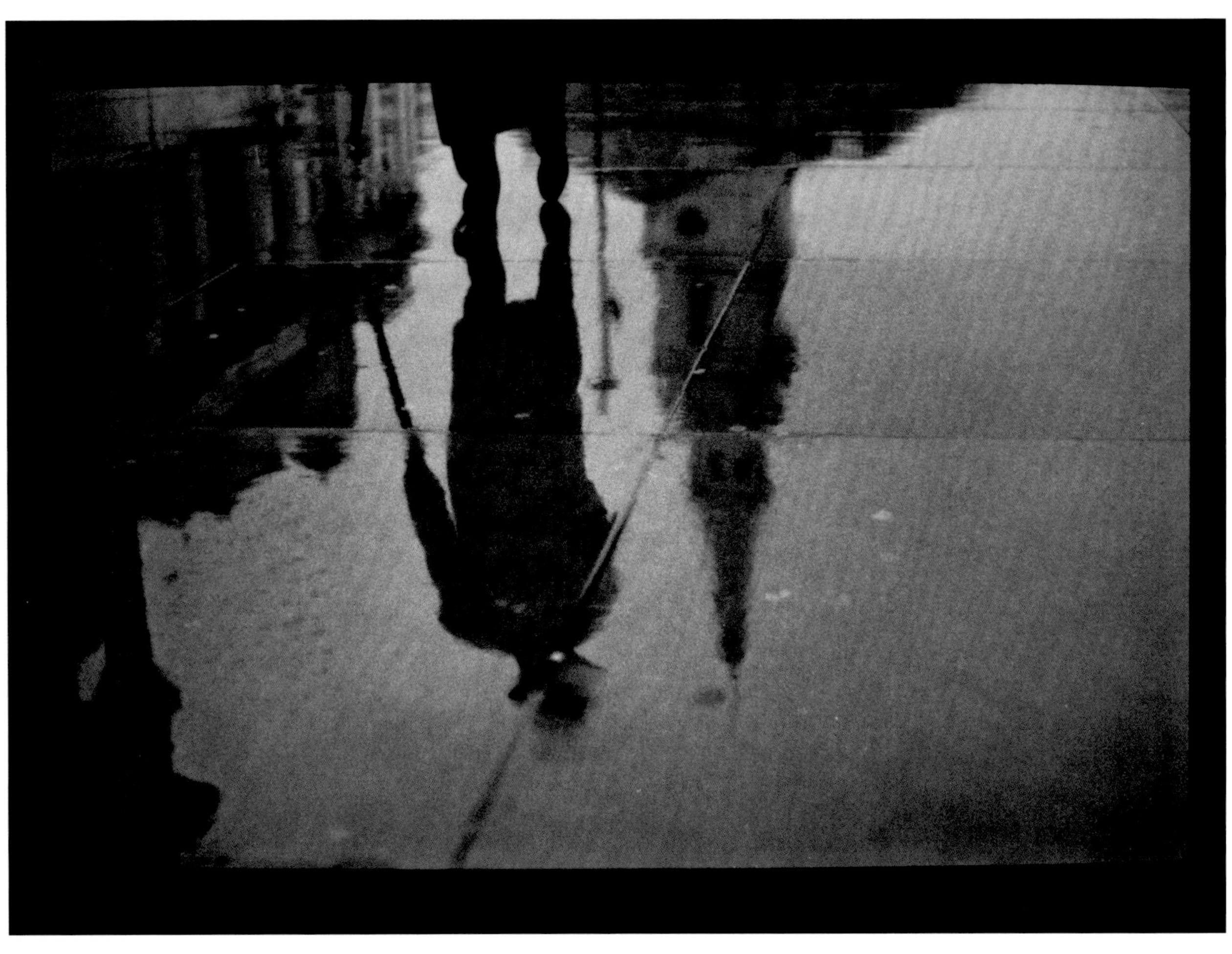

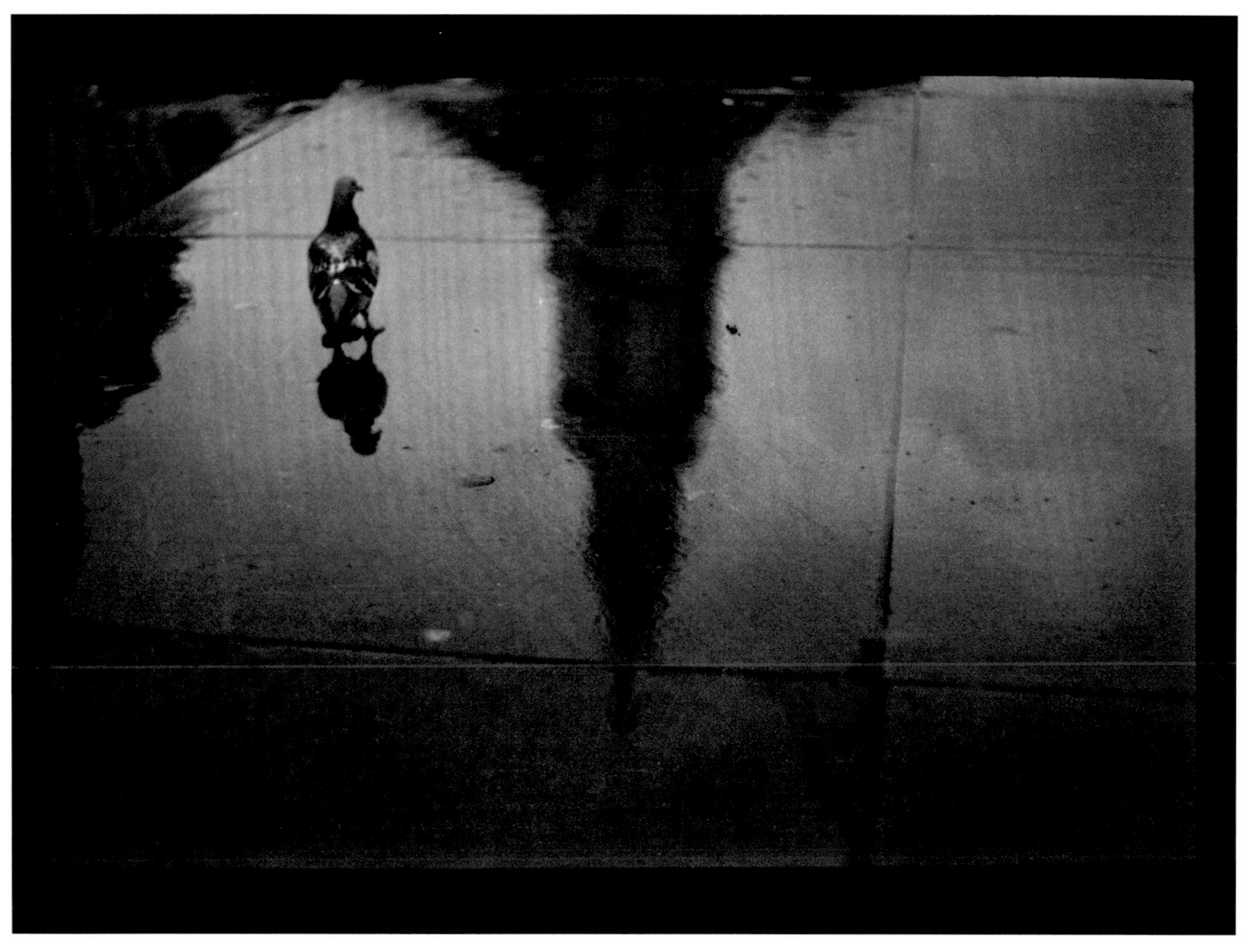

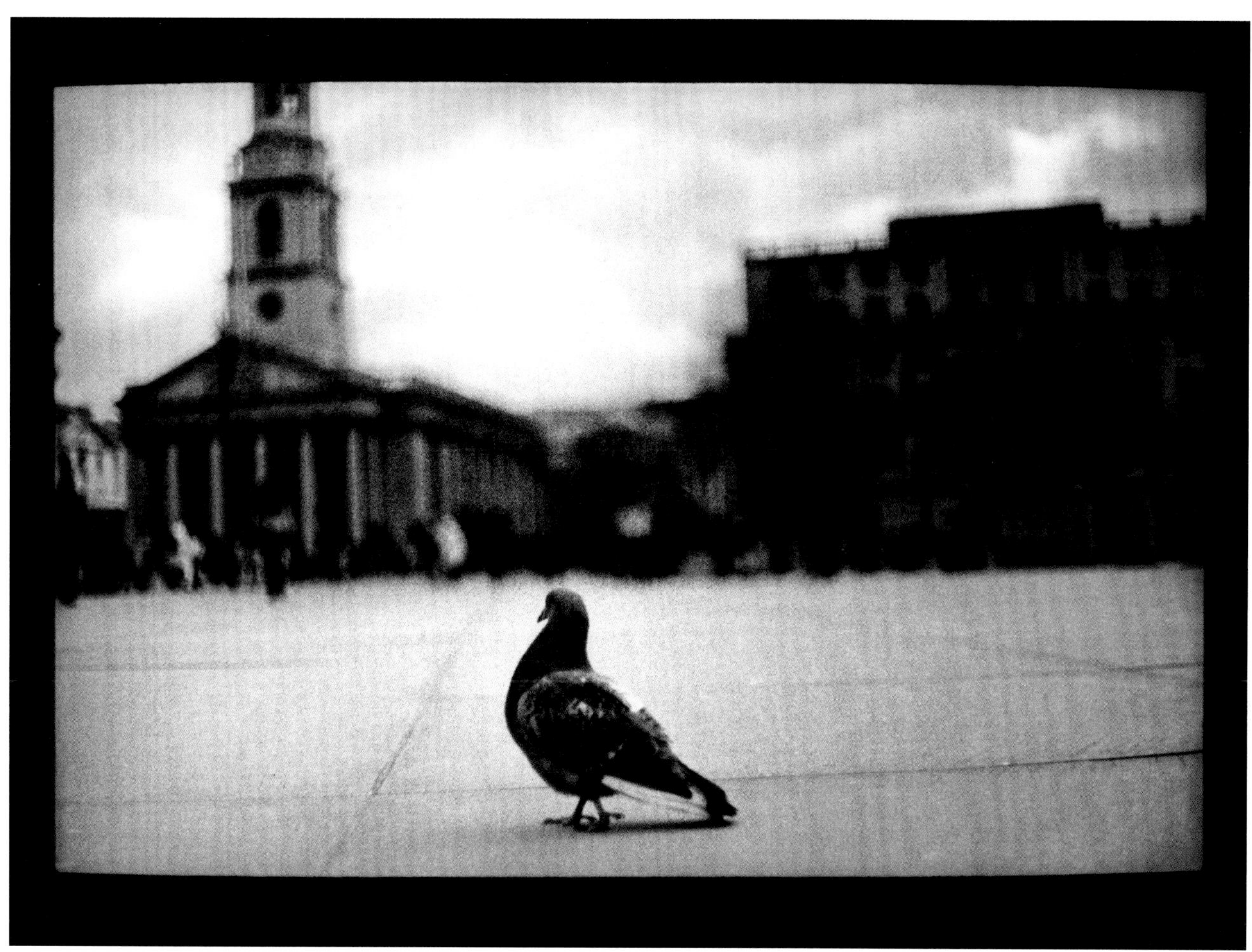

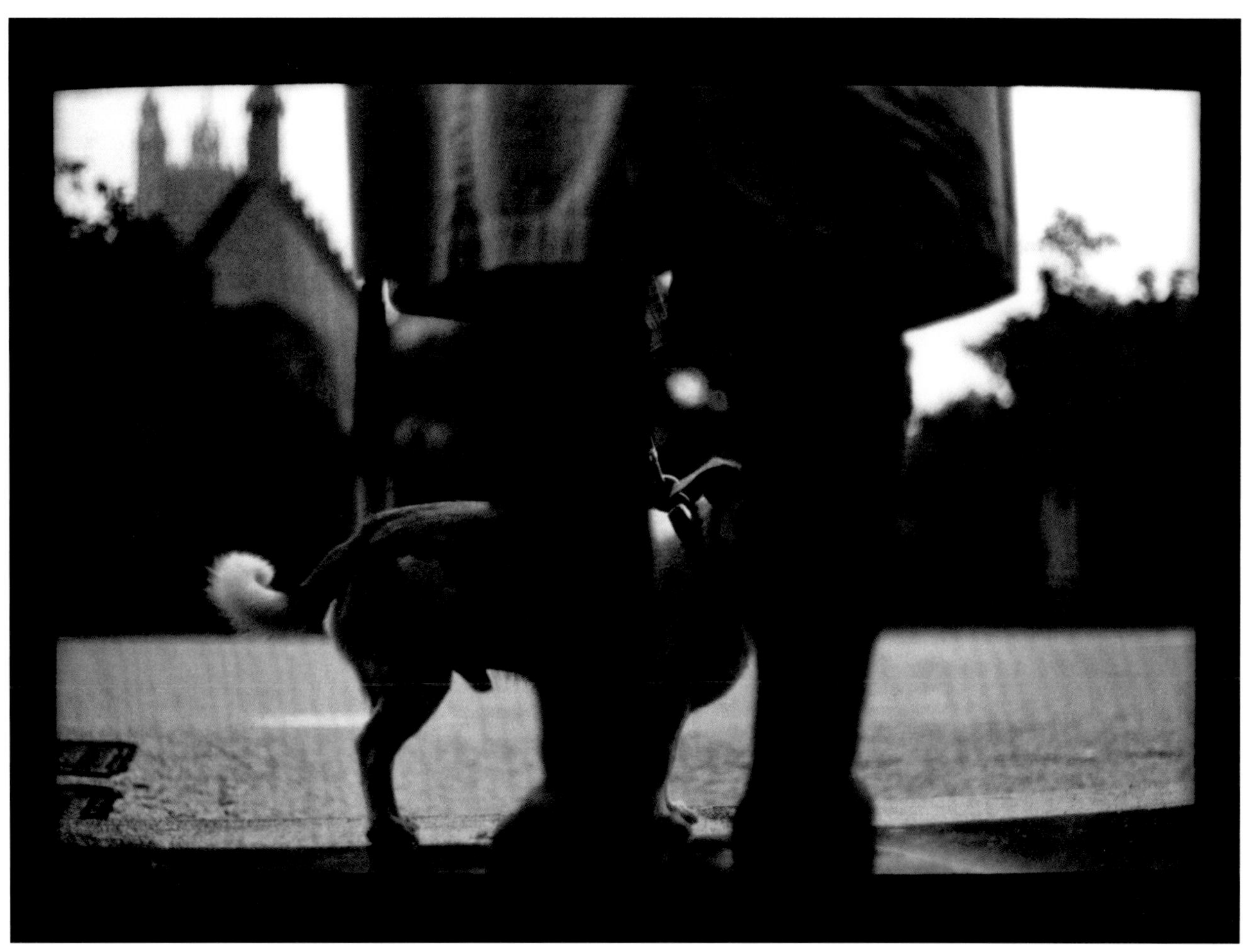

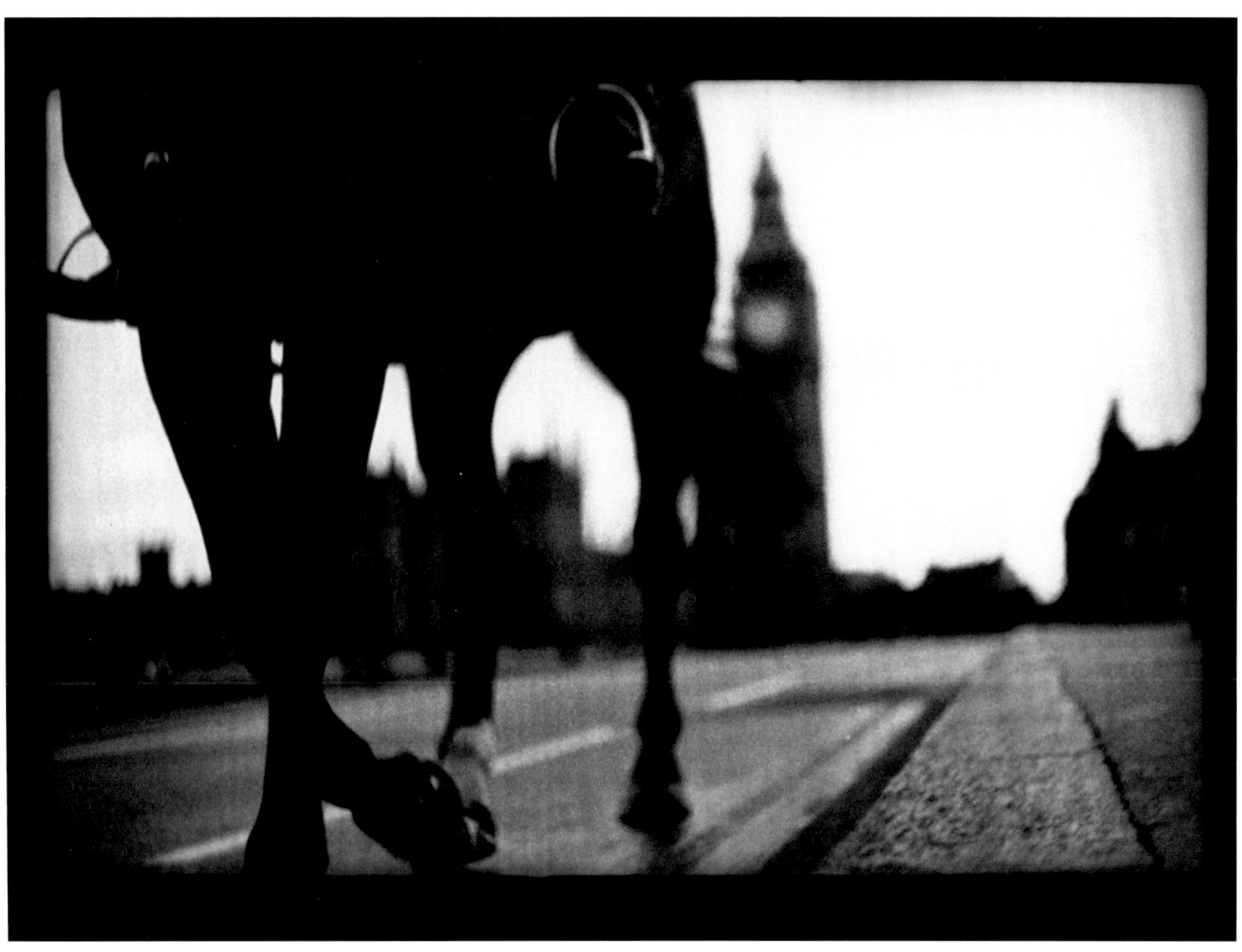

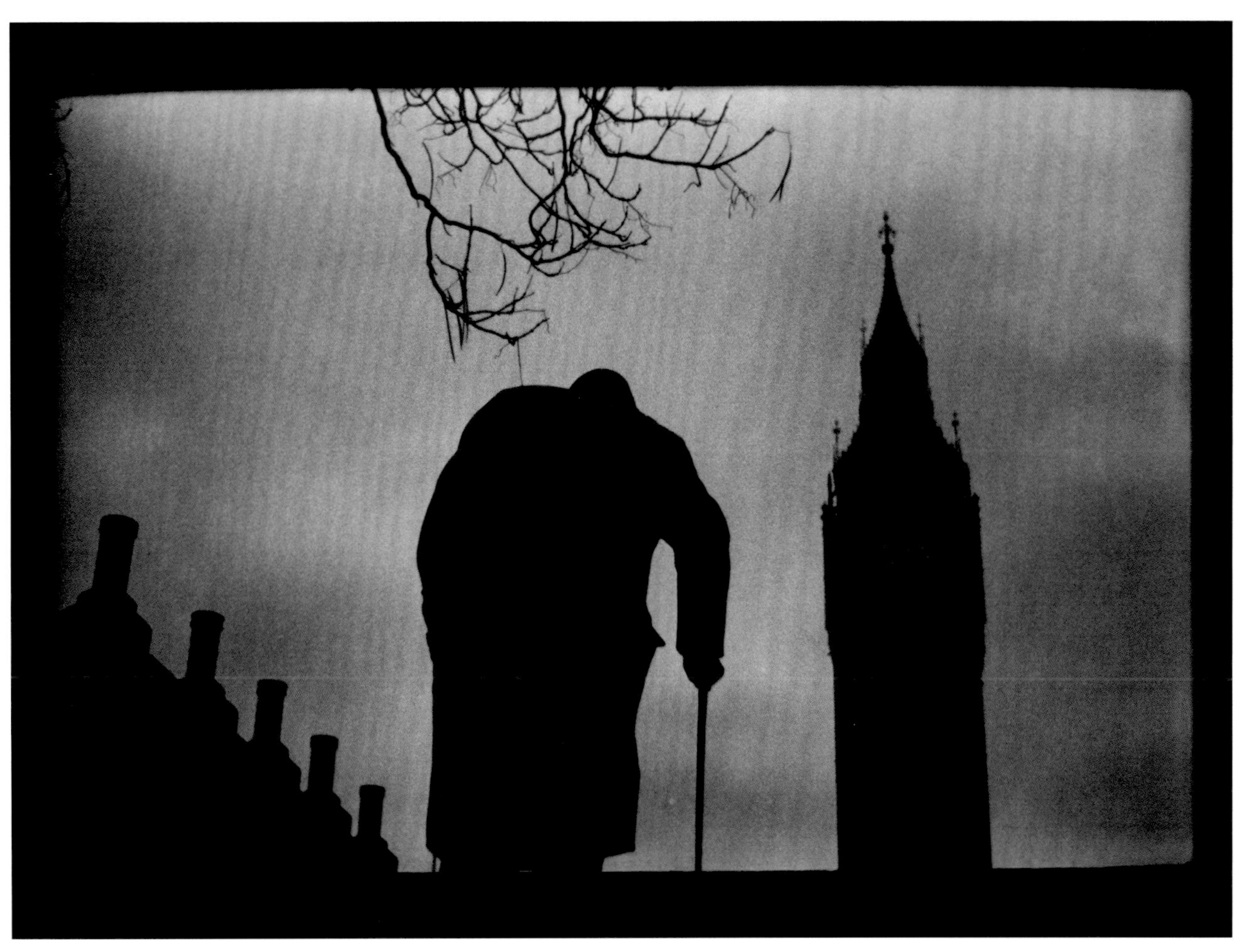

Go where we may, rest where we will,
Eternal London haunts us still.

Thomas Moore

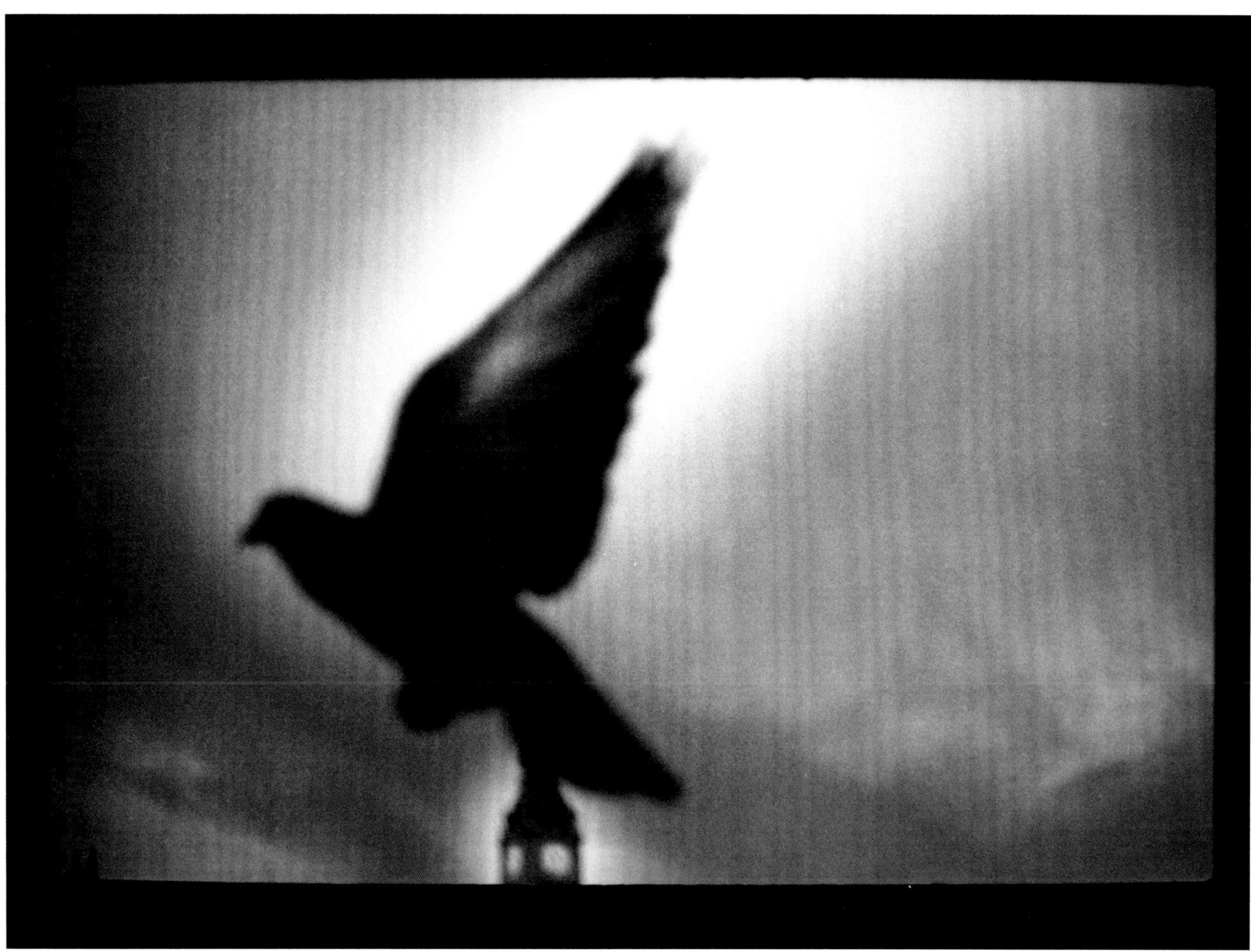

With thanks to

Dewi Lewis, Caroline Warhurst, Brett Rogers,
Gemma Barnett, Anthony Hartley, Anstice Oakeshott,
Shodor Uddin, Julian Page and Sharon Easterling.

Giacomo Brunelli

First reprint November 2016

First published in the UK in 2014 by
Dewi Lewis Publishing
8 Broomfield Road
Heaton Moor
Stockport SK4 4ND
England

www.dewilewis.com

For the photographs: Giacomo Brunelli
For this edition: Dewi Lewis Publishing

ISBN: 978-1-907893-52-0

Design: Dewi Lewis Publishing
Print: EBS, Verona, Italy